PORTLAND MADE

THE MAKERS OF PORTLAND'S MANUFACTURING RENAISSANCE

KELLEY ROY

WITH PEGGY ACOTT

First published in 2015 by Portland Made Press.

Text © Portland Made Press
Photography © Portland Made Press

Library of Congress Cataloging-in-Publication data available

Portland Made: The Makers of Portland's Manufacturing Revolution
By Kelley Roy with Peggy Acott

ISBN-13: 978-0692468920 (Custom)
ISBN-10: 0692468927

Cover Photos: Aaron Lee
Cover Design & Illustration: Jen Cogliantry

Editor: Christina Henry de Tessan, Girl Friday Productions

Book Design & Illustration: Jen Cogliantry
Book Photography: Aaron Lee
Additional ADX Photography: Josh Doll

Printer: Brown Printing, Portland, Oregon

Portland Made Press
417 S.E. 11th Avenue
Portland, Oregon 97214

portlandmade.com

ABOUT THE AUTHOR

Kelley Roy is the founder and owner of ADX and the Portland Made Collective (PMC). From working to grow American manufacturing to consulting with people from around the world to create makerspaces in their communities, Kelley has become a globally recognized leader in the American manufacturing and maker movements. She has a graduate degree in urban planning and an undergraduate degree in geological sciences, and, in 2010, coauthored *Cartopia: Portland's Food Cart Revolution*. Kelley is passionate about helping creatives hone their skills, start their own businesses, and make a living doing what they love.

ABOUT ADX

ADX is a hub for collaboration where individuals and organizations make and learn. By sharing tools, knowledge, and experience, we're doing things better—working together. Our makerspace, learning center, and custom fabrication shop allow anyone to bring their idea to life. In our fourteen-thousand-square-foot facility, high-profile designers work alongside students, retirees share their knowledge with novice builders, and entrepreneurs collaborate with hobbyists. adxportland.com

ABOUT THE PORTLAND MADE COLLECTIVE

The Portland Made Collective (PMC) is a digital storytelling platform and advocacy center for Portland's Maker Movement. PMC is a collective of over 500 members from around the Portland Metropolitan Area that generate tens of thousands of jobs and billions of dollars in economic activity for our local economy. As a social impact company, PMC is committed to providing Portland makers with opportunities to grow through media and marketing support, public education, promotional events, retail opportunities and other local partnerships. PMC member businesses includes those from fashion, food, and the home goods industry sectors. The online hub acts a resource for local makers both small and large and seeks to raise consumer awareness about all of the amazing things that are created here in Portland, Oregon. portlandmade.com

ACKNOWLEDGMENTS

When Kelly Rodgers and I wrote *Cartopia* it was a true team effort, with lots of sharing of tasks, writing assignments, review of each other's work and intense collaboration. So, I knew that with *Portland Made*, I would need to pull together a team that would help me get everything done on the incredibly short timeline I set for myself. People often say that I have unrealistic expectations. Or that my expectations are too high. To them, I say, "Stop setting the bar so low and reach for the stars." I like challenging projects, on tight deadlines. It pushes me creatively and keeps me focused on actually accomplishing what I have set out to do.

That being said, this book would NEVER have happened without the incredible guidance and direction of my editor Christina Henry de Tessan of GirlFriday Productions. She reminds me of a bootcamp trainer. *Write! Write! Write!* and then *Trim! Trim! Trim!*, so we end up with a beautifully sculpted story. I wanted to keep writing and trimming and sculpting but she finally made me put my pencil down and turn in my assignment. So thank you! You are a total rockstar and have been incredibly patient with me, the slightly neurotic perfectionist!

I am also eternally grateful to Peggy Acott, who helped me get as many interviews with as many makers as possible within our tight timeline. I kept saying, "one more," and she would always agree. Until she got a puppy and then I knew I was doomed (because I had a puppy too— classic Kelley move to get a puppy in the midst of so much work). Peggy's writing was so easy to edit and work into the book that I feel like I should be calling her my coauthor. Matthew Preston also helped early on with some of the initial research and writing and helped add a slightly sassy style to the book. To my two photographers, Aaron Lee and Josh Doll, well done sirs! The photos are absolutely gorgeous and beautifully capture the people, the materials, the process and the final products.

If you do not know Jen Cogliantry, you need to. She is one of the most incredible designers I have ever worked with. And she has recently launched a new line of beautiful fiber-based accessories, so you should check her out at jencogliantry-handmade.com. Jen was so incredibly patient with me during the design process and added her own touch with graphic elements that tie everything together.

And were it not for my incredible team at ADX, I could not have taken time away to reflect on the past five years and write this book. It was so incredibly important for me to not only take note of what I had created, but also to delve deeper into the stories of the people who make Portland so incredibly amazing. Thank you team, for holding everything together at ADX and for all that you do to help our members realize their dreams.

Thank you, glorious beauty that is the Oregon Coast. I spent a lot of time writing out at the coast and ol' mother ocean was a great supporter during the long, laborious birthing of this book. It is the ocean that keeps me going and reminds me how incredibly lucky I am to be here in this amazing place I have called home for the past 20 years.

Finally, thank you to ADX members and our extended family who are the Makers of Portland's Manufacturing Renaissance. This book is for you. Thank you for taking a chance, believing in yourselves and creating such beautiful handcrafted goodness. And thank you for allowing me to share your stories with the world.

DEDICATION
To my best friend Merle.

CONTENTS

THERE IS SOMETHING ABOUT PORTLAND

There is something about Portland, and I felt it when I first visited in 1994. I knew as soon as I saw the city from the top of the Fremont Bridge that I had found my new home. I had been planning to move to Seattle, but I instantly connected with Portland: the people, the place, the culture. Nestled compactly at the base of the west hills, with the beautiful Willamette River meandering through it and a stunning collection of bridges, Portland felt very European. The scale felt right; it was easy to navigate and the people were super friendly. It was grittier back then: the Weinhard Brewery occupied the center of the city, and the adjacent industrial area (now the exclusive Pearl District) was full of punk-rock art galleries, potholed gravel streets, and run-down warehouses used for band practice and after-hour parties. Back when nightly visits to venues like Satyricon, La Luna, Berbati's, and EJ's featured some of my favorite local musicians, including Hazel, Elliott Smith, Quasi, Sunset Valley, and so many more. I lived in the Division/Clinton neighborhood before it became one of the hottest restaurant rows in the nation—back when the Red Apple was the only grocery store; Reel M Inn, Dots, and the Clinton Street Pub were the only nearby watering holes; and La Cruda and Ruthie's were the only restaurants.

During my twenty years of living in Portland (excluding a few stints in Austin, Brooklyn, and Seattle), I have seen the city grow and attract creative people from all over the country. Drawn by Portland's reputation for a thriving start-up culture and can-do attitude, people are moving here

> **There is a certain quality to people who take these risks. One part resourcefulness and one part industriousness, with a dash of punk-rock, fuck-the-man scrappiness, it's a quality I adore.**

now, sometimes without a job, and oftentimes with a dream to start something of their own. Once they've arrived, many of them find themselves inspired by those around them and easily build a support network of like-minded people. There is a certain quality to people who take these risks. One part resourcefulness and one part industriousness, with a dash of punk-rock, fuck-the-man scrappiness, it's a quality I adore.

As urban economist Joe Cortright explained in an article in CityLab in response to an article in the New York Times,

Portland State University researchers Greg Schrock and Jason Jurjevich have shown, far from retiring, young and talented people coming to Portland are decidedly entrepreneurial. On average, they're 50 percent more likely to start their own businesses. And Portland ranks third nationally among large metro areas in the fraction of its college-educated young adults running their own businesses.

This entrepreneurship has been a genuine boon to local economic growth, as has the ease of attracting bright young workers from elsewhere . . . Metro Portland ranks ninth in the top 100 metro areas in economic performance according to the Brookings Institution, based on job growth, productivity, and the housing market.

Entrepreneurs are already contributing to the rapid growth in Portland's food and tech sectors, and the handcrafted goods industry is not far behind. It is the combination of these three industry sectors that is making Portland the darling of national and international media, investment, and tourism. Large troops of Japanese tourists are flocking here to experience our culture and buy our goods. There is now a Portland pop-up shop in Tokyo, and many Portland businesses have opened second locations in other cities around the country and are exporting their goods to locations around the globe, including Melbourne and Tokyo.

But Portland isn't just about experimental restaurants, handmade goods, craft brewing, and a funky food-cart scene. It also wins people over because of its proximity to nature—many who move here to start businesses cite the easy access to hiking and camping as one of their primary reasons for being drawn to Portland. People also seem to be attracted by the city's strong civic values. It may sound like a utopian fantasy, but the fact is that this is a city filled with people who care: about each other, about where their food comes from, about who made their beer and spirits and how, about how their transportation choices impact the environment, and about how much time they spend adventuring with friends. The facts bear this out. Portland has the highest bicycle ridership in the country, the highest concentration of craft brewers, one of the nation's most successful farmers' markets, and an incredibly active citizenry. We are voracious consumers of handcrafted, locally made goods and are outdoor enthusiasts, with an evangelistic drive to protect this place we call home.

Portlanders kind of have it figured out, and people across the country are catching wind of the Portland way of life. Whenever my parents visit and we go into a local coffee shop, they say, "Why aren't all of these customers at work?" Well, they are at work. Portlanders are redefining work. What it looks like. What it feels like. Where and how it happens. What it is. And people around the globe are taking notice. Portlanders are a purpose-driven bunch, and if one of us gets a thing in our craw, we're going to give it a go and see if we can make it work. While people have ideas everywhere, here's what sets Portland apart: when we ask for support from each other, we get it. And we're not afraid someone is going

Portlanders are redefining work. What it looks like. What it feels like. Where and how it happens. And people around the globe are taking notice.

We are playing in bands, starting our own line of leather goods, and writing books. We are designers by day, poets by night and snowboarders and surfers when the conditions are right.

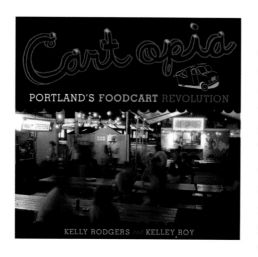

to turn around and steal our idea. Want to know what Portland's Intellectual Property law is? "Don't be a jerk. Don't steal other people's ideas."

Portland is often criticized for having a slacker attitude and poor work ethic compared with big cities like New York or Los Angeles. But I have a different perspective. Portlanders are the scrappiest, most hardworking and adventurous bunch of people I have ever been around. Portlanders are doers. We are not afraid to try and fail, and the relative affordability of the city makes such risk taking possible. We don't need huge amounts of money to start our business and live our dream. We work hard, but we know when to call it quits and enjoy ourselves. We support each other in our endeavors, and many of us have three or four things we do to make a living—our way. We are playing in bands, starting our own line of leather goods, and writing books. We are designers by day, poets by night, and snowboarders and surfers whenever the conditions are right. And we are able to do this because we don't need a lot of frivolous material items. Our consumer habits are different. We don't need to wear a new outfit every day so that we can climb the corporate ladder.

While people in larger and more expensive cities are clawing their way to the top (and barely getting by), we in Portland are sharing things in order to live the life we want to lead. Portlanders embrace the real sharing economy. From cars to tools to housing to work space. We collaborate on projects and bring our collective networks of support together to crowdfund our projects. We share knowledge, experience, and space so we can do the things that we love. As we learn from each other along the way, we make fewer mistakes, and we figure out how to create better things that last longer. Then we can go on to help others who are just starting out. Then we go camping.

As a result of this generous collaborative spirit and tenacious entrepreneurial streak, we have an incredibly strong network of creative people working together to make things happen. Like Paris in the 1920s or New York in the 1950s, talented creative types are constantly making connections over great food and drink and planning and scheming about new and interesting projects. Instead of feeling threatened by others, we feel inspired and motivated by the prospect of collaboration—we know that our network of friends and supporters is our biggest asset.

After moving back to Portland in 2008 and taking a look around at this fantastic energy, I quickly realized the potential of these expansive networks of creatives. I explored this topic through the lens of food carts back in 2010 while the idea of ADX was being conceived. ADX officially launched in January 2011 and opened its doors six months later. The original idea was to channel all of the amazing creative energy swirling around by bringing people from a variety of backgrounds together under one roof to share space, tools, and knowledge and to work together. By harnessing that energy and giving it some structure, ADX has helped to create new jobs; new product lines; new businesses; and new ways of thinking about art, design, and production. Since its inception, ADX has become a support system and hub for the new artisanal economy, which values well-made, handcrafted goods that support people, planet, and profit equally. ADX's mission is to elevate Portland as the creative capital of the world.

Today, ADX helps designers and makers of all stripes with all aspects of their business, whether they need help taking their products to market or creating profitable business models that lead to more and longer-lasting quality jobs in the new artisanal manufacturing sector. It also serves as a space for artistic exploration through both traditional and new technological mediums. ADX hosts poetry readings, music shows for all ages, art exhibits, meetups, and hackathons on a regular basis to keep the spirit of discovery and creative expression alive. The blending of artists, designers, and technologists under one roof at ADX is an ongoing catalyst for Portland's thriving artisan economy. In short, ADX is at the heart of what I like to think of as the Portland Renaissance.

Portland has a long history of industriousness and creativity, but in the past, artists and designers working in different specialties have tended to stick together: photographers with photographers, ceramicists with ceramicists, woodworkers with woodworkers. That makes a certain amount of sense, of course—those artisans can share tools and materials and speak the same language. But what happens when you bring artists and designers from all backgrounds together under one roof and give them access to tools and each other? And even more important, what happens when you bring young people into this environment and engage them with a new way of learning from each other and the community around them? I have been discovering the answers to these questions and many more since opening the doors to ADX in 2011.

I have had the good fortune of being at the helm of an extraordinary experiment in urban life. Portland is at the forefront of a new American manufacturing revolution, and ADX has been an important catalyst in shaping the handcrafted goods movement. I am constantly asked—by Portlanders, non-Portlanders, politicians, nonprofits, other creatives who want to start similar movements in their own cities—what this creative renaissance looks like. This book is the answer. ✂

ADX

IS A COLLABORATIVE
MAKERSPACE WHERE
INDIVIDUALS AND
ORGANIZATIONS MAKE
AND LEARN. BY SHARING
TOOLS, KNOWLEDGE,
SPACE, & EXPERIENCE,
WE'RE DOING THINGS BETTER
BY WORKING TOGETHER.

MAKERS GOTTA MAKE

WHY NOW?

AMERICA IS MAKING AGAIN

The main theme of the past twenty-plus years has been fast, cheap, and out of control consumption. Walmart's "Everyday Low Prices" summarizes this obsession. We are a nation that has been brainwashed into thinking that low prices are the only measure of value that matters. But there was a time in America when value meant something other than cheap. Back in the early part of the twentieth century, value meant high quality. Value meant long lasting. Value meant crafted with love and dedication and attention to detail. Clothes were made to last and shoes were made to be repaired, and broken things were fixed. It wasn't a disposable world; rather, it was one that valued longevity, frugality, and living within your means. Most Americans had lived through the Great Depression and many knew what it felt like to lose everything.

Sometime in the late seventies, cost became the only consideration and paved the way for poor global trade policies like NAFTA. The reasons behind the decline in American manufacturing are complicated enough to warrant their own book. However, it's well worth summarizing a few of the most alarming aspects of the global manufacturing shift in order to put Portland's local manufacturing renaissance in context. According to Randy Komisar, partner at venture capital firm Kleiner Perkins Caufield & Byers,

In the 1950s, one third of the American workforce was employed in the manufacturing industry; the economy not only supported manufacturing jobs, it thrived on the power of this sector. Since then, U.S. manufacturing has been in a sharp decline as overseas production has become the dominant choice for American companies. Since 2000, the U.S. has seen 5.8 million manufacturing jobs shift overseas.

The industrialization of our food products and the globalization of manufacturing (accelerated by policies like NAFTA) meant that manufacturers of consumer products could drive costs down. It didn't matter that these new products were poorly made, didn't last, and lacked artisanship. It didn't matter that women and children were working in unsafe factories that polluted local water systems. It didn't matter that people overseas were being exploited and that foreign governments were being bullied into deregulation by big corporate giants.

Consumers' new purchasing power allowed for the massive growth of retail giants like Walmart, Costco, and IKEA, and this in turn put pressure on distributors and, ultimately, on suppliers and manufacturers to provide goods at the lowest possible cost. Driven by a profit-first mindset, companies began to seek cheaper labor, cheaper material, and a manufacturing landscape with as little government oversight as possible. Many foreign countries were willing to court these eager suitors, and so began a mass exodus of American manufacturing to China, India, and Asian-Pacific countries.

This trend of driving costs down continued as the Internet opened the doors even wider and disconnected us even further from the process of making things and the people working in the manufacturing sector. The traditional retail experience in which we bought things from local store owners who specialized in and curated quality goods suffered as cheap chain stores took over. These stores are owned and operated by multinational corporations like Walmart, Costco and IKEA that pay people minimum wage and no benefits to sell poorly made goods manufactured overseas. We became blind consumers with no connection to the people or process of production, and the gap between rich and poor in the US and globally began to widen rapidly.

The huge leaps being made in technology, the continued subsidies for big oil and the rapid automation of manufacturing processes from the 1980s through the early 2000s also allowed for cheaper international communication, cheaper transport and a smaller labor force. Those changes, combined with the bullying of foreign countries by large multinational corporations to limit regulations, created poor environmental and working conditions that went mostly unnoticed by American consumers. As a result, the bulk of American manufacturing soon found itself overseas and went largely unregulated.

For years the manufacturing process was out of sight, out of mind, and the American people turned a blind eye to the reduced quality of goods being sold to them. With the Internet still rather primitive up through the early 2000s, a majority of people were unaware of how and what went into the products they were purchasing—the products had American corporate branding, and they were cheap and widely available. Comfort, convenience, and affordability were the buzzwords for several decades, and the how

The traditional retail experience in which we bought things from local store owners who specialized in and curated quality goods suffered as cheap chain stores took over.

and why of that comfort and cheapness went unquestioned. A massive boom of advertising reach, new research and marketing tactics, the rhetoric of politicians increasingly funded by corporate interests, and the many reforms in federal regulation and consumer protections all paved the way for an alarming—and unprecedented—mindset of rabid consumerism. People didn't know better. We were so busy working so that we could consume more that we failed to see what we were sacrificing: our own health, as well as that of our communities and our planet.

As the globalization of goods and services grew, economic reliance on local skilled artisans decreased, and high-quality craftsmanship became less and less valued. Shop class all but disappeared from middle and high schools and students who were once encouraged to learn trade skills were left behind. As a result, we have lost an entire generation of skills, craft, and artistry along with the apprenticeship programs that used to serve non-college-bound students. These days, students are told that college is the only option. We have failed our kids and are just now realizing the long-term economic impact of that as our population continues to be divided between the working poor and the super wealthy. We have lost our middle class and we have lost our connection to the value of making things with our hands.

As a result of all this, people have lost their understanding and appreciation of what actually goes into the products they are purchasing: Who is making the products? How much are those people getting paid, and what are their living conditions? What is the environmental impact on the places where the products are being made?

The rapid growth of the Internet suddenly made information more widely available, and the world started to feel smaller—with the click of a mouse, we could be apprised of events going on across the globe. More Americans were able to see what the factory conditions looked like in other

countries with no protections for people and no environmental regulations. Everything that was out of sight, out of mind was now visible—from the devastating contamination caused by the electronic waste we ship to China to the vast Chinese coalfields that fuel the world's growing demand for cheap goods to the poor working conditions in most third world countries where our big corporations hide from human rights and environmental regulation. Human rights groups now had a way to reach greater numbers of people, and corporate opaqueness became harder to maintain.

Then in 2008, the United States slipped into a recession and people began to grumble about the quality of the goods they were purchasing and the lack of middle-class, living-wage jobs. The recession shone a harsh spotlight on a way of life based on the soulless consumption of products that are hazardous to our health and on toxic food filled with pesticides and other chemicals that are not regulated overseas. Many began to think there had to be another way.

While big, greedy multinational corporations took advantage of the lack of regulations overseas, companies in Portland like Gerber Legendary Blades, Leatherman, Bullseye Glass, the Joinery, Chris King Precision Components, and others remained loyal to the their American workers and supply chains. They began to see a growth in sales and demand for high-quality American-made goods as the words "American Made" came to mean something to people, carrying more weight as a brand both locally and internationally. With the recent rise of crowdfunding platforms like Kickstarter and Indiegogo, supply and demand has begun to work its magic in the realm of American manufacturing and artisanal products. These, along with online marketplaces like Etsy, put more power in the hands of makers, who soon realized that they could use them to connect directly with customers. It was no longer necessary to make five thousand units of your product before you knew whether there was a market for it. Now you could make one, put it up on a crowdfunding site or online marketplace, market the hell out of it, and see how many consumers ordered it. In the past few years, sites like Crowd Supply and Betabrand have created even more streamlined models for taking products to market by helping makers with marketing, manufacturing, and distribution. There are many companies that find cost savings in keeping production local, especially when they want to put their values to work. They make smarter decisions that benefit everyone in the chain of production all the way through to the consumer.

The past few years have seen a noteworthy paradigm shift in American industry as the demand for locally made products increases. There is a growing trend for well-made, handcrafted goods produced by real people with a passion for what they do. These industrious individuals are making manufacturing sexy, and many people are gravitating to them and their products. Portlanders, along with makers in some of our more enlightened cities around the nation, are showing the rest of the country and the world how to focus on high-quality durable goods that are destined to become heirlooms instead of garbage.

People have also begun to realize that buying things from friends and neighbors they know and trust is much more rewarding (and safer) than going down to a sterile and impersonal big-box store. It is the emotional bond that forms during a direct transaction between consumers and makers that will keep the maker movement strong and headed in the right direction. Consumers have the power to change the conditions of production by touring local production facilities, asking lots of questions, and demanding higher standards. This type of accountability builds consumer trust.

These days, many consumers want to buy the story behind the product as much as the product itself. They realize that that story is an integral part of the final product, that individuality and uniqueness and the maker's vision are all valuable parts of the equation. Consumers are interested in learning about the people behind the products—and if they can meet them in person, then all the better, as explained by professor Jeff Cornwall at Belmont University.

"There's a growing dissatisfaction with the way of the last decade or two which has been—let's just outsource it and rely on large foreign manufacturers to take care of all of our needs," says Prof Cornwall. "If you look at some of the hidden costs that come about from trying to outsource, it's really resulted in much smaller cost saving than people first thought. . . . We don't have the mass market mentality in the US anymore."

Consumers are putting the focus back on quality, and they are demanding products that are ethically manufactured and locally sourced. This direct-to-consumer model also benefits makers, as more of the profit goes directly to them instead of a retail middleman.

Portland's maker movement is just beginning to engage consumers in a similar way as the

food movement has—where people have reacted to the industrial-food complex by getting to know their farmer, visiting farms to see how they were being operated, and joining community-supported agriculture initiatives to assist farmers financially with a prepaid customer base. People are hungry to learn how things are made and to directly support the makers of the products they buy. In response, many companies are opening up their factories for regular tours so that consumers can see "how the sausage is made" and then buy directly from them. Visible manufacturing builds consumer trust.

The desire for human connection and understanding about how things are made is starting a local manufacturing revolution that demands authentic and trustworthy interactions with real people who care about their communities, their cities, and the impact their choices have on people's livelihood and on the planet. These real people are the Makers of the Manufacturing Renaissance.

This desire for human connection and understanding about how things are made is starting a local manufacturing revolution that demands authentic and trustworthy interactions with real people who care about their communities, their cities, and the impact their choices have on people's livelihood and on the planet. Even large corporations are trying to get in on the act. J.Crew invested millions of dollars in the Madewell brand to appeal to this desire for American-made goods—even though most of its products are not made in the United States. And "stealth" Starbucks are opening locally branded coffee shops around the country that hide any connection to the corporate monolith. Much could be written about the dishonesty of such facades, but the point here is that this movement has enough momentum that even the country's corporate giants are taking notice. And consumers can smell the difference and know when they're being "local-washed."

Portlanders have staked their claim. We are the real deal. Our values are reflected in the products we produce with our very own hands. This is what other cities can learn from Portland: care enough to make a difference, and operate with transparency and integrity. This is an exciting moment in history—the revolution has undeniable and unprecedented momentum. Now it's about showing the rest of the country what a deeply interconnected maker movement looks like and tying it all together with good policies that support American-made goods.

WHY HERE?

PORTLAND IS MAKING IT!

Portland has been drawing creative, risk-taking adventurers to the city for most of its history, but they've been arriving in ever-greater numbers since the 1990s—and these numbers have positively exploded since the recession of 2008. With the tech, food, and maker movements drawing a wide spectrum of creative talent from across the country, the pioneering spirit and entrepreneurial energy are spreading like wildfire. The most common story I hear is that people want to trade in the rat race of the big city for the more balanced and affordable lifestyle of Portland. Many people are quitting their day jobs or dropping out of college to pursue their lifelong passion, whether that's craft brewing, fashion, home-goods production, farming, or furniture building. Many of these passions have turned into actual businesses, and Portland has gained national and international attention for its high-design and high-quality products. As artisanal manufacturing across all industry sectors continues to grow, Portland has suddenly found that it's the darling of the national maker movement.

Perfectly positioned between Seattle and San Francisco, Portland has always been overshadowed by its older sisters to the north and south. But several factors make it an obvious center of gravity for this artisanal renaissance. For one thing, Portland's relatively compact size and human scale makes street life and neighborhoods more vibrant and easy to navigate. People run into each other, meet their neighbors, and get involved with local businesses and community-development activities. Portland is a very friendly, civic-minded, and somewhat anti-establishment city, which is what gives it its independent streak. The renegades who settled in Portland instead of heading off to try to make it big during the gold rush years kind of bucked the norms and set the stage for future generations of hardworking industrialists.

Portland has always been a town known for wearing its principles on its sleeve, embracing al-

ternative ways of living and supporting people with a slightly rebellious spirit and a strong sense of individuality. While Portland's values-driven lifestyle has gained sometimes hilarious notoriety through shows like Portlandia, that sense of integrity and authenticity is a fact of life here. For every unicycle-riding, leotard-wearing, Darth Vader–masked, Dumpster–diving "weirdo" featured in Portlandia, there are another twenty hardworking, dust-covered, debt-ridden individuals busting their sweaty asses off to turn a dream into a living wage. And these hardworking folks deeply value collaboration, quality, and community.

Oregon's role in the food movement illustrates our principles and shows how powerful they can be. Oregon led the organic movement with a small group of forward-thinking farmers who developed Oregon Tilth in 1974. Considered an outlier in the early days, its work has increased awareness of the way we eat across the nation. In the same way that Oregon farmers raised public awareness around food, Portland's makers are engaging consumers about the products they buy. As an example, over seventy-five thousand people from all over the world have toured Portland's makerspace, ADX, since 2011, and those numbers are increasing by the day. Many manufacturing companies are opening up their factories for regular tours and selling their products directly to consumers from their factory stores. These direct purchases are the most beneficial for the makers, for our communities, and for our city. It is estimated that for every dollar spent on a direct purchase from a local maker, eight times that gets spent in the local economy. This means better schools, bustling main streets, and thriving communities. Portlanders continue to express their values through the power of their consumer choices.

Portlanders also have an incredibly rebellious, fun-loving spirit that meshes well with our creative endeavors. We're generally not in it for the money and tend to favor the unconventional over the nine-to-five corporate norm. Good friends, good beer, good weed, good music, good camping, and a good art are some of the ingredients we harvest to create the good life. Shirking the big fancy cars, expensive clothes, extravagant homes, and bougie lifestyles of those in more cosmopolitan cities like Los Angeles and San Francisco, Portlanders choose to spend their hard-earned money on doing and creating things. The ubiquitous bumper stickers "Keep Portland Weird" speak to our rebellious spirit and enthusiasm for avoiding the mainstream.

This trifecta—our relatively small, compact scale; our principled mentality; and our tendency to

embrace the quirky, unusual, and experimental—has made Portland the perfect breeding ground for a maker movement that celebrates handcrafted, artisanal, and entrepreneurial endeavors and supports the radical risk takers who believe in doing things better—and having fun while they're at it.

If Seattle and San Francisco are embracing technology with an aggressive "bro culture," then Portland is their more rebellious sister who believes in business that values art, people, and community.

Although the Portland business scene is often criticized by outsiders for not being cutthroat enough—not competitive enough, not moneyed enough—these folks are missing the point. That is not our goal and those are not our values. Those sound like values of an economy run by the Man, and it appears that Portland has a more feminist approach to doing business that just might reflect the future of our economy. If Seattle and San Francisco are embracing technology with an aggressive "bro culture," then Portland is their more rebellious sister who believes in business that values art, people, and community. Portlanders are deeply civic minded and have one of the highest rates of community participation in the nation. How shallow it is to think that business is only about making money. In fact, many of us fight for the underdog and protect the values that keep big corporate interests at bay. We're fighting hard to keep the city affordable to all.

Portland is increasingly exporting its way of life, most recently through its popular food and restaurant brands like Blue Star Donuts in Tokyo, Pok Pok in New York City and LA, and New Seasons Market in San Francisco. Our rock-star chefs are in demand across the country. And our food-cart culture launched a trend that has taken off around the globe. It's all evidence that these cities want in on our culture. Portland is being exported as a brand, and that's increasingly true of our artisanal products, too. We are seeing an increasing demand for Portland Made goods around the world, with most of the demand coming from Japan.

One step at a time, Portland is showing the nation, and the world, that hard work, passion, and a desire to live a fulfilling life is the future of success in business. A highly varied collection of small, artisanal manufacturers can drive a thriving economy that ws local culture and a lifestyle that is not only about consuming for the sake of it. Yes, there is a deeper point here. Companies with a set of shared values that transcend the almighty dollar bill can have a huge impact on the American economy.

THE TRAILBLAZERS

Portland's long history of manufacturing means that an extensive ecosystem of manufacturers with an incredible wealth of knowledge is already in place. Portland's new generation of makers can learn from what came before.

One of the founding fathers of Portland's manufacturing sector, Thomas Kay, a weaver from England who honed his skills in East Coast textile factories, came to Oregon in the late 1800s to establish what would become Pendleton Woolen Mills.

John A. Zehntbauer and Carl Jantzen founded the Portland Knitting Company, which would become Jantzen, in 1910. They made sweaters, woolen hosiery, and other knitted goods and sold them directly to consumers from their own retail location.

In 1939, Joseph R. Gerber started knife company Gerber Legendary Blades as a small-batch handmade cutlery factory. Today Gerber employs over three hundred people in its factory in Tigard, Oregon, and its knives can be found in thousands of retail locations across the country.

Another wave of creativity began in the late 1970s and early 1980s. Bullseye Glass was the dream of three art school grads who decided, in the summer of 1974, to set up shop in their backyard to make colored sheets for the stained-glass trade. Today Bullseye Glass employs over 120 people in their Portland, Oregon, factory and still produces glass one handmade sheet at a time. In a similar vein of artistic exploration leading to a full fledged manufacturing business, the Joinery, founded by Marc Gaudin, started as a one-man furniture repair and refurbishing business in 1982 that now employs over thirty people who design and build handcrafted furniture in its southeast Portland woodshop. The company's commitment to sustainability includes classification as a certified B corporation, use of 100 percent renewable power, and use of 100 percent locally sourced and sustainably harvested wood species for furniture making.

Founded in the same year as the Joinery, 1982, Pratt & Larson was launched by Portland artists Michael Pratt and Reta Larson. Located in the heart of the Central Eastside Industrial District, the company employs over eighty people and distributes its products throughout the United States and Canada.

PORT
LAND
MADE

KIRIKO

PORTLAND OREGON

KIRIKO

Kiriko was launched by Dawn Ynangihara and Katsu Tanaka at the 2012 Portland Bazaar. Dawn and Katsu started Kiriko to create items that tell a story. Their fabrics represent pieces of Japanese history and culture in which craft and quality were the objective. Each day they hope to create unique pieces that people cherish and hold on to. Kiriko use traditional, vintage and antique Japanese fabrics to create handmade accessories. All pieces are inspired by traditional fabrics and techniques.

TEXTILES TELL A STORY.

THE MAKER MANIFESTO

WE ARE MAKERS.
WE WORK TOGETHER AS A COLLECTIVE.
WE BELIEVE IN OURSELVES AND IN EACH OTHER.
WE TRUST THE CREATIVE FORCES WITHIN US
TO LEAD US THROUGH FAILURES AND TOWARDS
A MORE AUTHENTIC EXISTENCE. WE ARE A
COMMUNITY TIED TOGETHER BY THE TOOLS
AROUND US AND THE HANDS THAT GUIDE US.
WE ARE NOT CLAMBERING OUR WAY TOWARDS
FAME AND FORTUNE. WE ARE STRIVING, EVERY
DAY TO BETTER UNDERSTAND OURSELVES AND
THE WORLD AROUND US. WE ARE YOUNG AND WE
ARE OLD. WE ARE DOING WHAT COMES NATURALLY
TO US AND PUSHING OURSELVES THROUGH THE
DISCOMFORT OF THE UNKNOWN. WE SUPPORT
ONE ANOTHER AND ENCOURAGE OUR FELLOW
MAKERS TO PERSEVERE THROUGH SELF-DOUBT.
WE ARE STRONGER TOGETHER, AND THE BONDS
WE FORM MAKE THE WORLD A BETTER PLACE.
WE ARE HUNGRY FOR CREATIVE EXPRESSION.
WE ARE DETERMINED PROBLEM SOLVERS.
WE ARE MAKERS AND THIS IS OUR TIME.

MEET THE MAKERS

INSPIRING STORIES. BEAUTIFULLY CRAFTED PRODUCTS.

Portland is full of doers. We build, craft and create. We cut, weld and sew. We design. We manufacture. We work. We are Portland Made.

Portland makers cut across a wide variety of industry sectors. From food, bikes, fashion and home goods, to distilled spirits, recreation and music products. Makers in Portland are getting attention from the likes of Martha Stewart and her American Made Award, as well as from national brands like Williams-Sonoma and West Elm. These big corporate brands are looking for authentic local brands, and the benefit to local makers is instant exposure to a larger national and even international market.

Consumers are the biggest and best investors for Portland's Maker Movement, and we are all, at the end of the day, constantly consuming things. Everyday we all make choices about what to buy. Do we simply buy the cheapest item or do we buy something that is locally made and a little more expensive in hopes that it will last longer? If you have to buy 10 of the same thing in your lifetime because it is poorly made and breaks, is it really cheaper? What if you spend a little bit more money up front and buy something that is handmade by a local artisan that will last forever? It's better for our economy, our community and for good ol' mother earth.

The following is a handful of profiles about Portland Made companies and their founders, and provides a look at the range, depth, and scope of Portland's maker movement today.

Dan Schwoerer and Lani McGregor
BULLSEYE GLASS

FOCUS

FINE ART GLASS MANUFACTURING

The year was 1974. Stained glass was at a peak in popularity. It was also the time of Oregon's progressive "Bottle Bill," and so there was an abundance of recycled glass to be had. Three ambitious (some would say naive) art school graduates came up with the scheme to create a glass-making factory that would produce sheets of colored glass they could sell to stained-glass artists.

Did any of them have a background or knowledge in glass manufacturing? No.

This was the rather nebulous beginning of what became an internationally known, one-of-a-kind fine art glass-manufacturing company, which would break rules and break ground over the next forty years.

In 1979, enter German artist Klaus Moje, who for years had been trying to find a way to fuse a wide palette of colored glass together to create variegated objects without the incompatibilities typical of the glasses available from existing manufacturers.

The idea of "something that hadn't been done before" was intriguing to the Bullseye team, so they set themselves to the task. When they succeeded, it was a major turning point. Though the challenges of introducing entirely new material into the marketplace made for a few precarious years, the idea of "kilnforming" glass—fusing or molding disparate colors of molten glass and kilnfiring to create a finished product—caught the attention of artists around the world. Bullseye became the "owners" of the fusing process, and over the next thirty years artists of all backgrounds came to Bullseye to try out ideas and to use its manufacturing facility for large-scale public art pieces.

Bullseye gallery director Lani McGregor says, "Our glass chemist refers to it as 'the spiral.' Artists bring us ideas and problems. Sometimes those ideas lead to a new glass or a new process

"KIDS HAVEN'T YET LEARNED TO BE AFRAID OF GLASS; THEY'RE STILL CURIOUS AND OPEN TO EXPERIMENT WITH IT."

for using the glass." Bullseye now operates a gallery in northwest Portland to showcase innovative glass artists and manufacturing and also has gallery locations in San Francisco and New York.

But there is a new chapter ahead.

On January 1, 2015, Bullseye Gallery officially changed its name to Bullseye Projects, moving the focus even more toward collaborations and glass education for all ages. Bullseye Projects also opened a new learning studio and expanded its collaborations with schools, museums, and galleries across the United States and around the world, increasing exposure to the wonders of glass for all ages. McGregor is especially excited about the additional children's programs. "Kids haven't yet learned to be afraid of glass; they're still curious and open to experiment with it."

McGregor is excited and enthusiastic for the possibilities ahead. "Who knows what it will bring...but it's been forty years of 'who knows?' So why stop now?"

CLASS EXAMPLES
coldworking basics
glass fusing
advanced vitrigraph murrine
kiln as chisel
pate de verre
press mold method

LEARN MORE:
bullseyeglass.com / bullseyeprojects.com

MAKER PROFILE

Sam Huff & Jevan Lautz

TANNER GOODS

FOCUS

LEATHER GOODS

Their motto is simple: *Worth Holding Onto*. It reflects the foundational and personal philosophy of Tanner Goods founders Sam Huff and Jevan Lautz, and informs the way they have built their business. It's the triumvirate of "quality, longevity and value" that are interwoven in every Tanner product. "We feel that the philosophy of the things we make is important in life and relationships, as well as in products," says Huff, who himself rides to and from work on a bicycle that was hand-built in the 1980s, given to him by his father-in-law.

Both Huff and Lautz grew up in the small town of Sisters, Oregon, a vibrant community of craftspeople with an abundance and pride in quality handmade items. The two grew up steeped in the appreciation of everyday objects that carried both aesthetic and workmanship quality. Huff feels that what they do at Tanner Goods is "a way to get back to our roots."

Lautz's background was in sales, Huff's in product design. It was an ideal combination of skills and talents. In 2006, they started producing natural leather belts and bifold wallets in the bedroom space behind their first retail location in NW Portland.

Timing, as they say, is everything. In the mid 2000s there arose a trend toward "heritage leather goods," driven in part by an influx of money being spent on apparel and accessories by men. Lautz and Huff were able to successfully leverage their products into this movement. Their mission of high quality, locally designed and manufactured leather goods hit just the right note, and their business took off.

In the nine years since its inception, Tanner Goods has grown by an astounding 30-40%

"THE TWO GREW UP STEEPED IN THE APPRECIATION OF EVERYDAY OBJECTS THAT CARRIED BOTH AESTHETIC AND WORKMANSHIP QUALITY... TANNER IS A WAY TO GET BACK TO OUR ROOTS."

annually – a 150 square foot room and two friends has grown to a 10,000-square foot workshop and office space with a total staff of thirty-five; two retail outlets (one in Portland and one in Los Angeles); additionally selling wholesale to approximately eighty retail markets in North America, and another eighty in Europe, Australia, Japan, and South Korea.

Even with the growth and expansion, at the heart of their business there remains the handprint of the personal, the individual. They think of their production staff as craftspeople, not technicians; many of them have fine arts backgrounds, and are encouraged to give feedback and design ideas on the products they make. The entire company's operation – production, shipping, administration – is all under one roof.

This is important, intentional. They want to avoid the hierarchical separation of administration and production. As it is, there is a lot of exchange and communication between all the members of the company. As Huff says, "We own the whole process from start to finish," keeping it personal, authentic and consistent in quality.

What are their biggest sellers? The un-dyed, natural leather belts and wallets. Over time and use, these take on coloration unique to the owner by virtue of contact with natural human skin oils and general wear, so that no two are ever completely alike. Everyone's belt or wallet becomes the unique talisman of its wearer. The "aha" moments for Huff and Lautz are when (in New York or Japan or on airplanes, at trade shows) people show them their Tanner belt or wallet they've had for years.

LEARN MORE / tannergoods.com

MAKER PROFILE

Stefan Andrén

KROWNLAB

FOCUS

PRECISION METAL FABRICATION

Sometimes an artist's love of craft inspires creation, and sometimes it's motivated by disappointment at what's available. Sometimes it's a little bit of both.

Stefan Andrén moved to Portland in 2003 and decided he was going to design his own house. One of the many space-saving elements that he wanted to include in his home were sliding doors, but the options avaible on the market were really clunky and unrefined. So he decided to design his own.

He worked with local machinist and longtime metal worker Rob Roy, who helped him prototype a sleek, modernist, high-quality design. Stefan's home received attention from popular national design publications, and the phone started ringing off the hook. For a long time, Stefan simply explained that he custom-made the sliding door hardware and that it was not available on the open market. He thought this would make people go away, but they kept calling. So he took a closer look at the sliding door market and found that there were no high-quality systems out there. The lightbulb went off and Krown Lab was born.

Krownlab now markets three types of sliding door hardware, all of which feature exposed hardware, which appeals to those who want to make an architectural statement. "I like objects that are simple in the way they appear," he says, "and honest in the way that you can tell what something does." Stefan recently expanded his company into a large warehouse space in Portland's NW Industrial District, and there is no sign of things slowing down anytime soon.

Although it can be hard for a growing company to maintain its commitment to quality, Portland makers are committed to upholding these core values of honesty, integrity, and authenticity.

LEARN MORE / krownlab.com

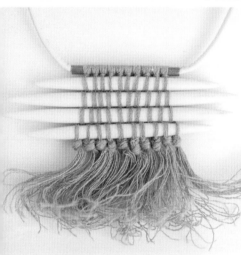

non-perishable goods

• 100% linen •

MAKER COLLECTIVES

The Makery stands by its motto: "Better together."

According to Julie Everhart, one of The Makery's member owners, the Makery is unique among the many shared artist spaces in Portland. While most artists pay monthly rent for a studio space, the Makery is operated by an artists' collective that uses the space as both a creative workspace and a forum for classes and workshops that are open to the public. There is a growing trend with Portland makers sharing large warehouse space. This is not only because real estate prices are rising, but a reflection of the values we have as makers to work together. The Makery stands by its motto....

Since 2014, the Makery has been the creative home to a mix of artists, including potters, a weaver, a soft-goods manufacturer, and graphic artists. "We have our own little ecosystem," says Everhart. Jobs—tasks involving social media, advertising, finances, and coordinating rent and other "shop mom" duties—are shared. The group meets regularly to check in and reorganize as needed. It's been "such a great little family from the beginning," she says. The Makery hopes to continue expansion, offering more classes and workshops and inviting nonmembers to participate, thereby creating a rich opportunity for local artists to learn from each other, as well as exposing the public to the wellspring of creative energy and knowledge that exists here in Portland.

THE MAKERY COLLECTIVE

PIGEON TOE /
pigeontoeceramics.com

KATIE ARMOUR /
katiearmourart.com

STUDIO OLIVINE /
studio-olivine.com

GRACE&FLUX / graceandflux.com

NON PERISHABLE GOODS /
nonperishablegoods.bigcartel.com

SACHA KNIVES /
sachaknives.com

ERIN GARDNER /
highsocietycollection.com

FOUR PLUS ONE PRODUCTIONS /
fourplusoneproductions.com

JOSH ANDERSON /
jlandersonart.com

HANNES WINGATE /
foreignservice.se

JESSICA WINGATE /
lecoulecou.com

EVAN SCHNEIDER

Kim Malek

SALT & STRAW

FOCUS

SMALL-BATCH ICE CREAM

The name Salt & Straw gives a nod to the rock salt that people used with old-fashioned hand-crank ice-cream makers to surround the container and chill the mixture inside; the straw was what the container of finished ice cream was wrapped in to keep it cold on hot summer days. Co-owner Kim Malek says the name is also appropriate because just as each hand-cranked ice cream was a small batch, Salt & Straw also produces small batches that change depending on the season.

Malek dreamed of having an ice-cream shop for nearly twenty years before Salt & Straw opened its doors. She had worked for Starbucks ("in the early days, where there were only thirty stores") and loved the sense of community engendered by the gathering of regular customers. She thought an ice-cream shop had a similar appeal—it would be a place where people could share a pleasant experience together. (Who doesn't love ice cream?) In 2011, she moved to Portland "for love." Her future husband, Mike, believed in her dream and finally convinced her to give it a try.

Meanwhile, her cousin Tyler had graduated with a degree in business in Seattle, but he was discovering his true passion was food. When Malek told him of her plan, Tyler "packed everything in his Subaru and moved to Portland" to help her.

What they soon discovered was that lots of people were enthusiastic about their dream and willing to put their time, energy, and expertise into helping them make it a reality. The strong collaborative energy in Portland gave them an idea for developing unique flavors of ice cream: "There are so many special, unique things being produced [in Portland] that to marry that with

"WE USE ICE CREAM AS A CANVAS FOR TELLING LOCAL STORIES."

ice cream is bound to equal interesting flavors," says Malek. So when Tyler wanted to try to re-create a sundae of sticky rice, fresh fruit, and ice cream that he had tasted while traveling in Asia, they contacted Andy Ricker, chef and owner at Pok Pok (one of Portland's most famous Thai restaurants), and asked if they could buy sticky rice from him. Instead, Andy invited Tyler over to the Pok Pok kitchen so Andy could teach him how to make sticky rice. Malek says, "Andy had just won a James Beard Award, and here he was, willing to teach Tyler how to make sticky rice for our ice cream." From there they sought out others to collaborate with, "using ice cream as a canvas for telling local stories."

Some of their favorite collaborations, however, have been with local schools. For the past four years, Salt & Straw has run a competition for new ice-cream flavors in the schools closest to their store locations. Three winners' creations get put on the menu, and the money raised from the sales of their flavor goes back to the school. In one instance, Vernon Elementary School was able to glean sufficient seed money to enable them to apply for (and receive) a grant to refurbish and upgrade their playground.

These collaborations are central to the heart of Salt & Straw. A strong business the number of people who regularly flock to the Salt & Straw locations, it looks like she has indeed realized her dream of community building through the magic of ice cream.

LEARN MORE / saltandstraw.com

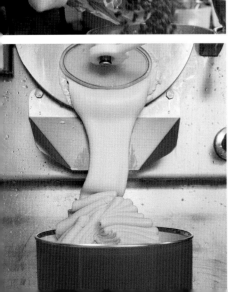

Sam Pardue

INDOW

HOME WINDOW PRODUCTION

Sam Pardue had a problem. He was living in a beautiful 1906 house with gorgeous wood-framed windows—windows that, unfortunately, leaked like sieves. He liked the original wavy glass panes, so replacing them with vinyl wasn't an option, and wood replacement windows were just too expensive. So he pondered and experimented, and one lucky day he opened his refrigerator and noticed the gasket around the edge of the door that seals in cold. He asked himself, Could an acrylic insert rimmed with a similar gasket work the same for windows?

And Indow was born.

That was 2009. As Pardue began to investigate, he quickly came upon a big challenge: due to ongoing foundation settling, windows in older homes are rarely square. So Sam developed a laser that could make accurate complex measurements in order to adjust the fit.

In 2010, Sam began beta testing in Portland, a town with a fast-developing urban core and homeowners who want to preserve their homes' appearances, while still implementing energy-saving solutions to their homes. It proved to be a steep but effective learning curve. "Being in business is what forced us to solve problems and get the necessary experience," Pardue explains.

A story in the Oregonian brought the company regional and national exposure. Today, Indow produces seven grades of handmade, US-sourced window inserts designed to filter varying amounts of light and noise. Indow's mission is to produce a product that maintains a home's structural integrity, preserves its beauty, and promotes an ethos of energy conservation and environmental awareness.

LEARN MORE / indowwindows.com

MAKER PROFILE

Erika and Sebastian Degens
STONE BARN BRANDYWORKS

FOCUS

DISTILLERY

When Erika and Sebastian Degens moved to Portland from the east coast in 1980, they were blown away by the variety and quality of the fruit that was being grown here. Inspired by such abundance, they threw themselves into canning, pickling and preserving fruit through the seasons.

According to Erika Degens, she and Sebastian occasionally talked about starting a business together someday, but work and family life predominated and the idea remained on the back burner for a while.

But in 2009, they started to think more seriously about starting a business. Sebastian had lived in Germany when he was younger and tasted the clear, bone-dry European brandy known as eau-de-vie, which was made by fermenting a variety of fruits. Finding very few equivalents here, he longed to bring this unique and flavorful style of brandy to local palates.

Things came together rapidly: Shortly after their kids headed off to college, they found the "perfect building" to house their distillery near four others in a part of inner SE Portland that has become known as "Distillery Row."

Their first product was a plum brandy, chosen because they suddenly had access to a large quantity of Italian prune plums. However, the fruit was frozen, and the thawing process—making the mash warm enough to feed the yeast—proved to be a challenge. The end results were mixed, but it was a crucial first step. Although Degens describes the episode as "a steep learning curve," they were on their way.

Soon they got into the rhythm of following the fruit harvest; and it became clear that their brandy

"SOON THEY GOT INTO THE RHYTHM OF FOLLOWING THE FRUIT HARVEST; AND IT BECAME CLEAR THAT THEIR BRANDY OFFERINGS WERE GOING TO FOLLOW THE SEASONS."

offerings were going to follow the seasons. In order to develop a consistent, year-round presence, they added whiskey to their offerings, which they made with flour from local Bob's Red Mill. And because elements of whiskey and brandy also go into making fruit liqueurs, they added those into the mix. This proved to be a good move for two reasons: One, it takes about twenty pounds of fruit to make 375 ml. of brandy, versus only three pounds of grain to make twice that volume of whiskey, which made their entire operation more cost-effective. Two, the public wasn't yet that familiar with their European style of brandy, so offering more familiar products of exceptional quality would draw customers who could then be introduced to the brandy. They've been successful at getting the word out—and getting people to try their brandies—through their tasting room near the Brooklyn rail yard, their booth at several area farmers markets, and Distillery Row's Passport Program.

Sebastian and Erika were recently lauded in Portland Monthly Magazine for being "not afraid to follow their curiosity." Degens says they have had a lot of fun experimenting with different flavors and combinations, including local hazelnuts, haskap (an Oregon-grown berry in the honeysuckle family, with a taste that's a cross between a blueberry and a cranberry) and spelt whiskey. Their employee Andy Garrison also adds his own creative curiosity when it comes to whiskey: Both a unique Oregon Bourbon and a Graetzer Rye are in the process of aging as of this writing.

"We are open to making a small batch, one-of-a-kind product, maybe only done once," Degens says.

LEARN MORE / stonebarnbrandyworks.com

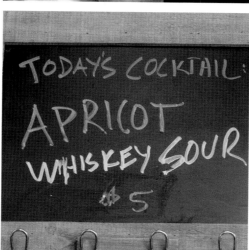

TODAY'S COCKTAIL:
APRICOT
WHISKEY SOUR
$5

STONE BARN
BRANDY
WORKS

THE
FASHION INDUSTRY

Portland's fashion scene is making a big splash nationwide. As of the writing of this book, Portland boasts four Project Runway wins, including Leanne Marshall (Season 5); Seth Aaron Henderson (Season 7); Gretchen Jones (Season 8); and most recently Michelle Lesniak (Season 11). Outdoor apparel has thrived here for years with the sustained growth of large companies like Nike, Norm Thompson, and Columbia Sportswear, as well as relative newcomers like Nau, Keen, and SKORA. But all of these companies face huge challenges to manufacturing in the United States, primarily due to bad trade policies that made it cheaper to produce goods overseas where there are limited environmental and labor laws.

The US textiles industry has all but disappeared, but there are two Portland companies, Portland Garment Factory and Spooltown, that are committed to bringing textile manufacturing back to the US and back to Portland, and they cannot keep up with demand. As a result, designers are finding it almost impossible to produce their work locally. In fact, the demand is increasing so rapidly that there is a call within the industry to create a fashion incubator, similar to what ADX does for craft goods: a place where fashion designers can share tools, order materials in volume, share professional-development resources, and work together to help each other be successful. An incubator like this could include a contract, small-run production team and an associated workforce-training program that could help grow the local fashion industry, enabling it to compete with other cities in the United States. The challenges are numerous, but an impassioned group of local designers and determined industry leaders are trying to make it happen.

Marjorie Skinner has been studying the indie fashion scene in Portland for more than a decade. Currently the managing editor of the Portland Mercury and author of its weekly Sold Out column on local fashion and retail, she has followed and reported on the progress and maturation of this segment of the Portland maker movement. She says she has definitely seen some changes in that time—not so much in the number of indie designers but in how they approach their work.

"Ten years ago people were experimenting at making a living," says Skinner. Fashion designers typically came from an arts and crafts, fine arts, or self-taught background; their experience was heavy on the artistic and creative aspects of the profession, less so on the business end of things. But over time designers grew more determined to transform what they had considered strictly a fun, creative venture into an economically viable and competitive career. "The conversation got more sophisticated," Skinner observes, and designers started to identify where they wanted to go and what they needed to get there. She sees this change particularly in the designers' approach to business and marketing, which is becoming "more savvy, more clean, more professional." This new focus has resulted in a marked increase in the overall quality of clothing design and production.

Back in the early 2000s, designers relied exclusively on a network of home sewers for the production of their garments and accessories. Designers kept their sewers a closely guarded secret to preserve their availability in the face of growing demand. Many designers used Etsy as their main portal for sales and required only small batches of a few designs. Because the minimum production requirements of large manufacturers were greater than these small makers needed to produce, they could not get their items produced.

Correctly seeing the need for a "middle ground" scale of production, Portland Garment Factory opened in 2008. The home sewers still had (and do to this day) plenty of work with small-batch production and one-of-a-kind, specialty-tailored garments, but Portland Garment Factory provided an important stepping-stone for indie designers who wanted to increase the availability of their product lines.

For the fashion industry as a whole, the challenge for the future will continue to be one of availability of adequate means of production: manufacturing in this industry is facing the same challenges as other realms, in that a large number of the workforce is at or nearing retirement age, and there aren't enough young workers training to take their places. Companies like Portland Garment Factory and Spooltown are playing a vital role by enabling designers to continue to have their garments and accessories made here in Portland.

MAKER PROFILE

Sara Tunstall & Dana Hinger
SPOOLTOWN

FOCUS

SMALL-RUN SOFT-GOODS FACTORY

Sara Tunstall and Dana Hinger, the co-owners of Spooltown, have an incredible amount of energy, enthusiasm, and confidence. Spooltown, a small-run soft-goods factory, has gone through some big changes since 2013. Their business has been on an upward trajectory that Hinger describes as like "riding a wild elephant." It led them to move from their shared warehouse location on North Williams Avenue to a warehouse in the inner Southeast's light industrial district, a space twelve times larger—an open expanse of sixty-five hundred square feet—and they say they can already feel themselves "almost out of space."

The workspace houses sixteen to twenty employees at any given time; they now are able to produce sewn soft goods for eighty to one hundred clients a year. "We would love to talk with everyone," says Tunstall, amazed by how many people are out there with good ideas and a drive for making. "But there are simply not enough hours in a day." So over the past year and a half they have been refining their space, staffing, and processes for the services they offer.

Spooltown is in a uniquely niche manufacturing market, especially in the Pacific Northwest, and being based in Portland has its advantages and challenges. "People here are doing things differently," says Tunstall. "The approach to making is from the ground up, rather than from the top down," meaning that there are no major institutions driving manufacturing; Portland's creative impetus is from individual and small-company makers and designers who just "stand up and start making things." But while this innovative and grassroots approach to its maker movement is invigorating, the lack of a built-in infrastructure like that which exists in Los Angeles and other major garment and accessory production cities is a major challenge. It is hard to navigate as a production business here without that sort of fundamental support chain. "You can't just go out

"THE APPROACH TO MAKING IS FROM THE GROUND UP, RATHER THAN FROM THE TOP DOWN, MEANING THAT THERE ARE NO MAJOR INSTITUTIONS DRIVING MANUFACTURING; PORTLAND'S CREATIVE IMPETUS IS FROM INDIVIDUALS AND SMALL-COMPANY MAKERS AND DESIGNERS WHO JUST 'STAND UP AND START MAKING THINGS.'"

and pick up sewing machine parts," for example. But this is where Hinger and Tunstall want to be. Here they can help provide a sense of community and viable local jobs while keeping alive their important mission of making American manufacturing visible (a twelve-foot aluminum garage door has been replaced with a glass roll-up door that allows those passing by to see the making). But maybe most important, they can help new designers with developing the skills and knowledge they need to achieve successful manufacturing of their product.

This education component is fundamental to Spooltown, and the need was apparent when, two years ago, they offered a workshop on "How to Work with Manufacturers." They expected about twenty people to attend but were astounded when more than 150 showed up and they had to turn people away. Clearly, Tunstall and Hinger had found their niche. But even with the considerable expansion that has occurred (and which doesn't show any signs of slowing), the two are cautious. "We don't want to become a faceless factory where we don't know our employees." They are pursuing the goal of maintaining a slower, steady and sustainable growth, in part made up of a core of ongoing and repeat clients. And though they had originally thought Spooltown would be a much more regionally based business, makers and designers from all over the country and internationally are now regularly contacting them. They have clients in several states from coast to coast, as well as in Vancouver, B.C.

LEARN MORE / spooltown.com

MAKER PROFILE

Brett Binford & Chris Lyon

MUDSHARK

FOCUS

CERAMICS MANUFACTURING

Brett Binford fell in love with clay at the age of five while working on his dad's kick wheel in the family basement. He didn't really consider a career in ceramics until a high school art teacher suggested it. "I kind of laughed," Binford remembers. But soon he realized that there were many career paths in clay, from gallery artist to teacher. "This could be my life," he thought. "I don't have to give it up when I graduate high school."

After studying art at Alfred University, Binford moved to Colorado to work for an established ceramicist. There he met Chris Lyon, who had also been introduced to ceramics at an early age and refused to give up his passion after high school. Before long, their mentor came to rely on the pair, and from the studio's ongoing soundtrack centered around Frank Zappa's "Mud Shark" came the inspiration for Mudshark Studios, which opened in Portland in 2006. "Clay is referred to, loosely, as mud," Binford explains, "and a shark being a sort of a predator, but looking for mud or feeding on mud, and that's how we feed ourselves—with mud."

After outgrowing a basement in northeast Portland, Mudshark moved into a seventeen-thousand-square-foot space in 2012 and expanded from eight to twenty-seven employees in a single year. The company now produces ceramic light fixtures for Schoolhouse Electric and Rejuvenation, as well as countless bowls, vases, and other items for independent designers around the country. In 2012, Martha Stewart named Mudshark one of ten recipients of her American Made Award.

Along the way, Binford and Lyon got business help from Portland Community College's CLIMB

"WE'RE ALL TRYING TO FIGURE THIS OUT, AND IT'S A MATERIAL THAT'S CHANGING, AND THERE ARE ALWAYS PROBLEMS, AND THINGS TO SOLVE."

Center and Mercy Corps Northwest. "We didn't know how to read a profit and loss statement," Binford remembers, "and we felt very naive on the business end. We just knew how to make things." These days, the Mudshark team shares its knowledge of the business of ceramics production with its designer clients. By advising a client on how a design can be subtly altered to make it more production friendly, Mudshark can sometimes cut the initial investment in half and therefore substantially lower retail price. "That could be the make or break to why a customer would buy or not buy your object," he says.

This kind of knowledge sharing helps everyone involved, Binford says, and reflects a sense of community he's seen throughout the ceramics world. "We're all trying to figure this out, and it's a material that's changing, and there are always problems, and things to solve." Mudshark has also been the beneficiary of helpful advice from more experienced ceramicists in Portland. "Even though we're a business," he says, "they'll just open their doors, open their heart, open their minds to helping. I think that's something really special."

LEARN MORE / mudsharkstudios.com

THE NUMBERS

The growing national and international attention Portland is gaining is definitely having an impact on the local-goods market. Although the rise in local manufacturing doesn't appear to have an impact on the GDP at the national level, there's ample evidence that small artisan manufacturing is having a real effect on Portland's economy. In 2014, Portland State University professor Charles Heying and research assistant, Stephen Marotta, conducted a survey of Portland Made members and the following is from their report:

INVISIBLE ECONOMY:
90% of the businesses surveyed were not included in any national databases. This means that this part of our economy is not being counted.

IMPACT:
The 126 members of the Portland Made Collective employ an estimated 1083 persons and generate revenues of $263 million.

* AS OF THE WRITING OF THIS BOOK, PMC HAS OVER 500 MEMBERS

** IT IS ESTIMATED THAT THE PORTLAND REGION HAS OVER 10,000 MAKERS.

MOSTLY YOUNG:
Eighty-two percent (82%) of all enterprises have been in operation 10 years or less, sixty-three percent (63%), five years or less.

BIG HITS & LONG TAIL:
Three (3) enterprises, that have been in operation for thirty (30) years or more, produced ninety percent (90%) of the revenues and seventy percent (70%) of the jobs. The lesson is not to ignore the numerous small young enterprises but to nourish them. Two (2) of the three (3) large enterprises, that have such an outsize impact, were started in small studios by founders trained in the arts, with a passion for their craft and the ability to turn that passion into something substantial.

SWEET SPOT:
When enterprises reach the threshold category of $500,000–$1 million in revenues, they make a dramatic shift from part time to full time employees. Below that revenue threshold, the balance between part time and full time employees is roughly equal, above the threshold, the ratio of full time to part time is five to one (5:1).

HOLE IN THE MIDDLE:

We discovered an exceptionally small number of enterprises in operation in the middle range of years, and a total lack of enterprises in the middle range revenue category. While this may be an artifact of the data, we prefer the explanation that periods of innovation and enterprise occur in waves. One wave in the late seventies spawned a wave of artisan/makers like Bullseye Glass, Pratt and Larson Tile, and the Joinery. The 2000s brought the next wave of artisan and makers. In between these two fertile periods, is the "hole in the middle," a transition period where there were few enterprise foundings.

61% POSITIVE REVENUE GROWTH:

Respondents reported very positive revenue growth with an average of sixty-one percent (61%) cumulative growth for the last three years. Estimates varied by size of enterprise, but surprisingly, the fastest growth was not in the smallest enterprises. Enterprises with revenues of $50,000–$100,000 report nearly doubling in size over the last three years.

ARTISANS & MAKERS:

When asked to rank their identity preferences, respondents clearly preferred the role of maker and artisan over entrepreneur or business person. The preference for maker/artisan may suggest that respondents value their skills in producing well-made handcrafted goods over maximizing financial returns.

BEYOND LOCAL MARKETS:

As expected PMC members rely on local markets, with forty-six percent (46%) of sales generated in Portland and another sixteen percent (16%) from the Northwest. But surprisingly thirty percent (30%) of reported sales came from the US, outside the Northwest, and eight percent (8%) were international.

CHALLENGES:

Respondents identified marketing and product development as the most important challenges and administration the least.

SUPPORT:

Why go it alone when you can have a whole community behind you? Portland Made is a collective of over 500 members and subscribers from around the Portland Metropolitan Area that generate tens of thousands of jobs and billions of dollars in economic activity for our local economy.

MAKER PROFILE

Shannon Guirl

CARAVAN PACIFIC

FOCUS

HANDCRAFTED LIGHTING AND ACCESSORIES

A huge fan of mid-century American design, Caravan Pacific owner Shannon Guirl launched a successful Kickstarter campaign in 2011 in order to start a lamp business. Her lamp designs have a slightly modernized twist of color that complimented the classic proportions of the original style.

As her business grew, she was determined to maintain her original made-by-hand aesthetic—even though some are constructed with as many as twenty-five individual pieces. She now has two part-time assistants to help meet the challenge of going from making one lamp at a time to as many as two hundred in a single month.

In 2013, she moved her operation into a 7,000-square-foot "creative studio collective" warehouse space called The Makery. Located in industrial North Portland, it is – one of several maker-collectives that have sprung up in Portland in the last few years. Guirl knows how tough things can be for individual makers trying to get started in the marketplace. "Learning how to jump those hurdles is easier in a community" where you can share ideas and information.

"Portland's maker community is so welcoming and nice," Guirl said. From the beginning, she found the Portland makers and small manufacturers to be generous with their knowledge and their time. She loves to tell the story of going to a manufacturer of hand-turned wood products, since she wanted even her lamps' wooden components to have a handmade aesthetic. "The wood turner community is pretty insular," she said, because it is such a specialized skill and a relatively small group. She feared they might not be receptive to her ideas. But she needn't have worried:

> ## "Guirl knows how tough things can be for individual makers trying to get started in the marketplace. 'Learning how to jump those hurdles is easier in a community' where you can share ideas and information."

"Here's these older guys who have been doing this for years, thinking it's pretty cool that here's this chick who is interested in what they do and appreciates their craft."

Going forward, Guirl plans to work on new lighting designs "to keep challenging myself." She would also like to do more education—not only teaching lamp-making, but also highlighting some of the stories of the mid-century designers who have inspired her on a blog, She believes it is important to share these stories with her own generation so that this important design movement doesn't get completely lost to modernism.

"It's like having a dialogue with history," says Guirl.

LEARN MORE / caravan-pacific.com

Scott Miyako & Alex Pletcher

PORTLAND RAZOR COMPANY

FOCUS

HANDCRAFTED STRAIGHT RAZORS

Scott Miyako and Alex Pletcher moved to Portland from Los Angeles in 2014 after hearing about and visiting ADX. They were looking for an opportunity to start a new company based on their passion for straight razors. After taking a leap of faith and making the move, Portland Razor Company was born, and there has been no looking back.

Scott has a long history of building and has made everything from custom cabinets and furniture to bicycles and knives. When he purchased his first straight razor in 2012, he discovered that not only are most straight razors imported but they are prohibitively expensive and mostly inaccessible to all but hard-core enthusiasts. Portland Razor Company has changed that, by making beautiful handcrafted straight razors that are affordable.

ADX has been instrumental in Portland Razor Company's success. From providing affordable space and tooling, to exposing their company to an extensive network of global media. "ADX has helped build the business in every way," Scott says. "Without it there would be no way to show up to a city with absolutely nothing and immediately have a working shop."

Portland Razor Company has experienced such rapid growth that they moved out of ADX and into their own space just down the street. They are hiring more blade smiths and exploring other complimentary product lines as they continue to grow, and are receiving accolades from straight razor enthusiasts all over the world.

LEARN MORE / portlandrazorco.com

THE MAKER MOVEMENT

K-12
EDUCATION

VOCATIONAL
SCHOOLS / INCUBATORS

**LIBRARIES
MUSEUMS**

MAKER
SPACES

COLLEGES
UNIVERSITIES

**SUPPORT
SERVICES**

JOBS

MAKERS /
MANUFACTURERS

NEW
BIZ

CONSUMERS AS INVESTORS

THE
MAKER ECOSYSTEM

From makerspaces, maker-collectives and incubators to academia, vocational schools, museums and libraries, the maker ecosystem is a vast and interconnected web of partnerships. Shop class and the arts have been dismissed as not necessary for the new technologically advanced and knowledge-based economy, and were cut from educational institutions at all levels (to the detriment of those who learn by doing and creating).

The maker movement has been building over the past few years as people remember the importance and value of learning and working with their hands.

The maker movement is reconnecting the arts, technology and industry, specifically through the world of manufacturing, and is likely the thing that will help our economy onshore and re-shore the jobs associated with making products again.

At a hyper-localized level, the maker movement supports artists and creatives from a wide range of industries, including food, music, home goods, fashion, physical technology and more. It is deeply connected to the Do It Yourself (DIY)—or what we now call Do It Together (DIT)—movement, which involves learning how to grow your own food, pickle and ferment, sew and stitch, weld, build, and so on. The Maker Ecosystem includes makers and the network of support around them, all of whom are contributing to the rise of artisanal manufacturing.

It is the support systems within this ecosystem that are allowing the maker movement to thrive, grow and feed a new manufacturing economy.

MERCY CORPS NORTHWEST / mercycorpsnw.org
OREGON MANUFACTURING EXTENSION PARTNERSHIP / omep.org
PORTLAND COMMUNITY COLLEGE / pcc.edu/climb/small-business/growing
ALBINA OPPORTUNITIES CORPS / albinaopportunities.org
COMMUNITY SOURCED CAPITAL / communitysourcedcapital.com

WHAT IS A MAKERSPACE?

A SPACE FOR MAKING

A makerspace is a place where people come together to use, or learn how to use, a wide variety of traditional and more technologically advanced tools to create an original project or product. It is a community gathering space for artists, designers, and explorers to share their craft, problem solve, and innovate and incubate new works. It is also a teaching and training ground for the next generation of entrepreneurs and manufacturers. From the novice ("I have never built anything before") to the expert ("I have been making since I was five years old") and everyone in between, makerspaces are a melting pot of local creative culture. It is remarkable to see what happens when you put people with different areas of expertise—architects, videographers, nurses, software developers, bankers, electrical engineers, sculptors, teachers, contractors, web designers, accountants, fashion designers, writers, graphic designers, poets, plumbers, musicians, and more—together under one roof and give them affordable access to tools and professional resources.

A common misconception is that a makerspace is

just about technology and 3D printers. Technology alone does not make a makerspace. Technology is just one of many tools. Although we should not ignore technology, the focus of makerspaces should be on bringing people together to learn and share skills. Makerspaces should be about creating a space for human interaction—because it turns out that when you put a bunch of people from a variety of backgrounds together in one space with a bunch of tools and various materials, they get super creative and innovative. They can solve problems together and accelerate solutions to pressing issues in their communities. Whether they are sharing materials, harvesting scraps from each other's projects, or creating first-generation prototypes and amazing works of art, there is a synergy that can't be found when working in isolation.

A common misconception is that a makerspace is just about technology and 3D printers. Technology alone does not make a makerspace. Technology is just one of many tools.

Why go it alone if you can have a whole community behind you? Visitors often comment that makerspaces are like their art and design studios in school, back in the day, except open to the public. Anyone with an idea, some curiosity, and a willingness to take a chance can join. Makers work together to challenge themselves and each other to produce the most beautiful products possible. On any given day, I witness our members' commitment to learning and their willingness to share knowledge with each other. The informal, unstructured learning is probably the most valuable piece for people. The back and forth dialogue, exchange of ideas, constructive critiques, and ongoing problem solving all reflect the philosophy of lifelong learning that makerspaces are here to support.

Portland makers work in a wide range of mediums—textiles, ceramic, wood, metal, glass, plastic, electronics, local farm-fresh ingredients, water, paper, and more. They use complex equipment like letterpress machines, woodworking equipment, winnowers, sewing machines, oscilloscopes, TIG welders, blenders, ovens, bottling stations, and more. The raw materials and equipment for some of these undertakings can be very expensive—which often prevents people from even taking the first step. Makerspaces overcome these barriers by providing shared access to space, tools, and professional business and financial resources.

With their extended network of partners and resources, makerspaces are the critical ingredient for

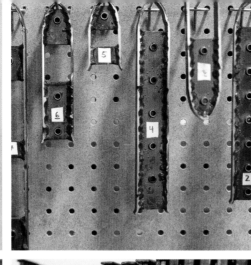

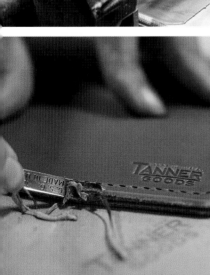

any local maker movement. They nurture new product lines by supporting designers, prototypers, fabricators, manufacturers, business coaches, marketing gurus, and financial wizards. Makerspaces provide assistance and a network of resources as designers go through the process of prototyping, taking a product to market, and developing a viable business. It's also much easier to take a risk when you have the support of an entire community of aspiring entrepreneurs by your side.

With their focus on collaboration, makerspaces are a critical part of the sharing economy. Their motto might be "A rising tide lifts all boats." The people who join ADX, Portland's maker-space, vary in their specialties and expertise, but they all share a commitment to doing some-thing with meaning and purpose; they are deeply engaged and care about learning, discovery, self-reliance, and community resilience. They are rugged individuals who play well with others, and they are reshaping the way we think of manufacturing. And it turns out that sharing tools and knowledge changes behavior—people realize that they can share other things, too. In that sense, makerspaces are pioneering not only a manufacturing renaissance but also a new ap-proach to ownership and community.

Designers and makers use makerspaces to prototype new product ideas, and with the help of crowdfunding platforms like Portland-based Crowd Supply, they can easily test the mar-ket to see if there is a demand for their product. Once they have proven there's a viable market, they need to figure out how to meet growing demand over time. Designing for a manufactur-ing process involves an understanding of how the product is made so that an efficient and cost-effective process can be cre-

As one of the nation's top makerspaces, ADX is where you come to make it yourself, learn how to make it, or hire someone to make it for you.

ated to produce larger volumes. Will designers and makers be their own manufacturer, or will they hire a contract manufacturer to produce their work? The answer depends on how involved they want to be in the production of their work. Artisanal production involves a process that creates objects at higher volumes while retaining a handmade quality. Manufacturing oftentimes involves moving to a production method that takes a handcrafted item out of the hands of the maker. We are lucky in Portland to have a wide range of local production facilities that will work with makers to retain the quality and values that are essential to their products.

Working at the intersection of so many industries –arts, technoogy and manufacturing–the maker movement is well positioned to help our economy onshore and reshore the jobs associated with making products again.

Working at the intersection of so many industries—the arts, technology, and manufacturing—the maker movement is well positioned to help our economy onshore and reshore the jobs associated with making products again.

As one of the nation's top makerspaces, ADX is where you come to make it yourself, learn how to make it, or hire someone to make it for you. Having all three activities happening under one roof creates a varied and dynamic environment. One of the critical ingredients missing from most makerspaces is an in-house design, fabrication, and manufacturing department that provides services for people who don't want to make a product themselves. Most of our clients are very busy business owners in other creative industry sectors—they may be restaurant owners or brewers, architects or tech companies. This business-to-business exchange has huge multiplier effects across the local economy—something not to be ignored by elected officials and economic-development leaders. It is estimated that for every dollar spent buying locally made goods eight times that gets spent in the local economy.

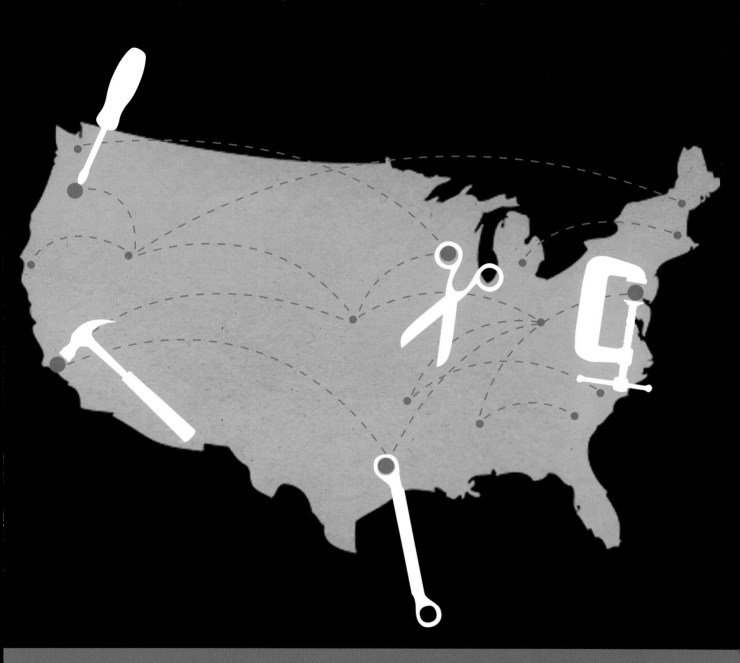

BUILDING THE NETWORK

ARTISANS ASYLUM / artisansasylum.com
TECHSHOP / techshop.ws **MAKER WORKS** / maker-works.com

BUILDING THE NETWORK
MAKERSPACES AROUND THE COUNTRY

Makerspaces come in many forms, and they continue to evolve as the maker movement grows. Artisan's Asylum, which opened in Somerville, Massachusetts, in 2010, uses a nonprofit model and depends heavily on volunteers, donations, and a pro bono board of directors. They received significant financial and staff support from the city of Somerville, including assistance finding affordable real estate. They have over 500 members, 170 studios, and 200 storage options that can be used to store materials, tools, and projects in process.

In contrast, TechShop uses a for-profit franchise model that has had varying success. While some of its outlets seem to be doing well, others shut their doors soon after opening. The first TechShop location was opened in Menlo Park, California and has since moved to San Carlos, California. It has eight locations across the United States and is actively seeking investors to expand into two additional US cities and to international locations. TechShop tends to be more tech focused and has a more corporate suburban office park feel than other makerspaces.

Ann Arbor–based Maker Works is more similar to ADX. It operates on a for-profit model that emphasizes community building as well as entrepreneurship and educational classes. Like ADX, it began in 2011 and is now offering "How to Start a Makerspace" workshops for people wanting to start their own.

The Steel Yard in Providence, Rhode Island, has been operating as a nonprofit since 2001. Its founders originally envisioned the space as "a sponsor and catalyst for innovative approaches to urban revitalization, arts promotion, workforce development, and community growth." steelyard.org Their programming focuses on education, workforce training, and fabrication projects across a wide range of mediums.

But it is still not easy, as the folks at Makerhaus in Seattle found out. They tried to implement a similar model to ADX but ended up closing their doors after only eighteen months. And TechShop is still trying to figure out the right model as it continues to open and close franchise locations in cities across the country.

Interestingly, all of these spaces—and most other makerspaces—were started by men. This may make some sense, because many of these spaces are started by people who are makers themselves, and the maker industry has been largely dominated by men. Fortunately this is changing. We are proud in Portland to have a makerspace started by a woman (that's me!), and a maker movement with many women founders and CEOs. We believe this brings a different sensibility and a more inclusive and collaborative feel to our facility and our community. These qualities are the future of our economy.

MEMBERSHIP *levels*

COMMUNITY - $50/month
Includes access to THE BRIDGE and community workspaces. Purchase Shop Passes for access to WOOD SHOP, METAL SHOP and the CRAFT LAB.

CRAFT LAB - $80/month
All benefits of the Community Membership, plus unlimited access to the CRAFT LAB. Purchase shop passes to access WOOD SHOP and METAL SHOP.

FREE-TIME - $150/month
Full access to all shops after 5pm on weekdays and all day on weekends.

UNLIMITED - $200/month
Full access to all shops during all open hours, including THE BRIDGE, METAL SHOP, WOOD SHOP and CRAFT LAB.

coming soon...
a new
TOOL+SHOP Orientation
for both
WOOD+METAL
one time $10 fee

NEW MEMBERS: Required
OLD MEMBERS: Strongly Encouraged

✱ STAY TUNED FOR DETAILS ✱

UPCOMING EVENTS

☆

Design your very own learning experience with

One on One INSTRUCTION

With a talented ADX maker

☆

CONTACT
Classes@ADXPortland.com
TO GET STARTED!

→ MADE HERE! →

Make your own @ADX

we have the TOOLS.

we have the CLASSES.

You have the AMAZING IDEAS.

WORK IT HARDER
MAKE *it* Better
DO IT FASTER
━━━ MAKES US ━━━
STRONGER
Our Work "IS NEVER OVER"
— DAFT PUNK —
MADE @ ADX

CUBE CLASSES EVERY WEEK!

Ask us about a
DAY of BUILDING

INSTAGRAM!
FACEBOOK!

1
2
3
4
5
6
7
8
9
10
11
12

WHAT IS ADX?

A COMMUNITY OF THINKERS AND MAKERS

It's almost difficult to think back to a time before ADX was part of the Portland landscape, but just a few short years ago our industrial creative space didn't exist. Influenced by an article in the New York Times describing the success of a Brooklyn workspace called 3rd Ward that acted as an incubator for new businesses, I recognized the potential for something similar here in the Northwest. I hoped to create a place for creative people from all industries to work on and craft their ideas and to provide the resources necessary to turn those ideas into actual businesses. I came from a business and community-development background with deep values in sustainability, affordability, and the power of the common man (and even the underdog to some degree). ADX seemed like just the sort of place where I could put my values to work.

Since opening in June 2011, ADX has facilitated a number of amazing fabrication projects from many of Portland's most influential designers and makers—alongside new work from emerging talent. We've also established a wide network of local enthusiasts eager to participate in and support our endeavors. ADX's membership base is a diverse cross section of experiences, backgrounds, and skill levels: high-profile designers work next to students, retirees share their knowledge with novice builders, and professional projects come to life next to those of hobbyists. In short, ADX has become a Portland institution where independent builders, designers, and creators of all kinds can gather, share ideas, and develop new skills.

But ADX has a complex business model with a lot of overhead that includes space, staff, and expensive tools. By diversifying our revenue stream across three distinct programs—member-

ADX also supports makers who are just starting out, including adults who are breaking into a new industry and students who have never been exposed to entrepreneurial activities in the manufacturing sector.

ship; design, fabrication, and manufacturing; and education—we've reduced the risk somewhat and managed to create a stable business model. While other makerspace models rely heavily on membership and education, ADX counts on a strong in-house design, fabrication, and manufacturing department to bring financial diversity to the business model. This department also helps makers get their products to market in a cost-effective way.

The ADX design, fabrication, and manufacturing team includes three full-time project managers and fifteen to twenty part-time designers, fabricators, and technologists. ADX is capable of fabricating a variety of goods for clients big and small nationwide, from tap handles for Hood River–based brewery Pfriem to a four-story interactive, arduino-controlled chandelier in a Denver apartment building to privacy huts for the internationally renowned tech company Airbnb. There is no limit to what the ADX design, fabrication, and manufacturing team can build.

While this business-to-business support is crucial to building a strong local economy, ADX also supports makers who are just starting out, including adults who are breaking into a new industry and students who have never been exposed to entrepreneurial activities in the manufacturing sector.

Today, ADX offers hundreds of classes and workshops per year, has over 250 members (most of whom are small businesses and product developers), hosts people from around the world on tours of our space three days a week, and works with clients from around the country on a wide array of products. Since 2011, we have seen over seventy-five thousand people come through our space. We have helped dozens of crowdfunding campaigns; assisted over two hundred businesses through their initial phases of growth; engaged over one thousand students ages five to twenty-two in hands-on learning; and hosted thousands of people for art exhibits, design shows, dinner events, live music shows, poetry readings, and nonprofit fund-raisers. We are a modern-day version of Andy Warhol's Factory studio, without all the drugs and pretentiousness. Our cool factor is our scrappy, hardworking, get-it-done attitude. Our rallying cry: Stop talking and start making!

One of the most exciting developments has been the connections ADX has forged throughout

A makerspace is at the center of a web of creativity that includes academic, institutions, industry, museums, libraries, nonprofits and small businesses.

the region. In addition to the connections ADX fosters when individuals work side by side, ADX also has strong links to other institutions, and these affiliations help create a resilient support network. ADX is working with MadeHere PDX to sell Portland-made goods and with the Equity Foundation to provide scholarships to those in need of financial assistance so they can gain access to ADX resources and programming. This interconnectivity and generosity of spirit and prioritizing of community is a powerful catalyst for people just getting started. A makerspace is at the center of a web of creativity that includes academic institutions, industry, museums, libraries, other nonprofits, and small businesses. Makers and their extended network of educational institutions, trade schools, design companies, art collectives, galleries, manufacturing partners, and retailers are now commonly referred to as "the maker movement."

ADX continues to get more and more media attention as the maker movement spreads across the globe. ADX has been featured in many Japanese publications, including Popeye magazine, and on the United Kingdom's Channel 4 alongside Portland Razor Company. It has been featured in national stories in Sunset magazine, Kinfolk, Metropolis, and the Wall Street Journal, as well as on CNN's United Shades of America and NPR's State of the Re:Union. And it has been covered regionally in 1859 and the Oregonian and on Oregon Public Broadcasting's State of Wonder, as well as locally in the Portland Mercury and the Portland Monthly and on stations KGW and KATU. The maker movement is gaining traction and piquing the interest of people from a wide variety of backgrounds all over the world.

It truly takes a village to make a maker movement.

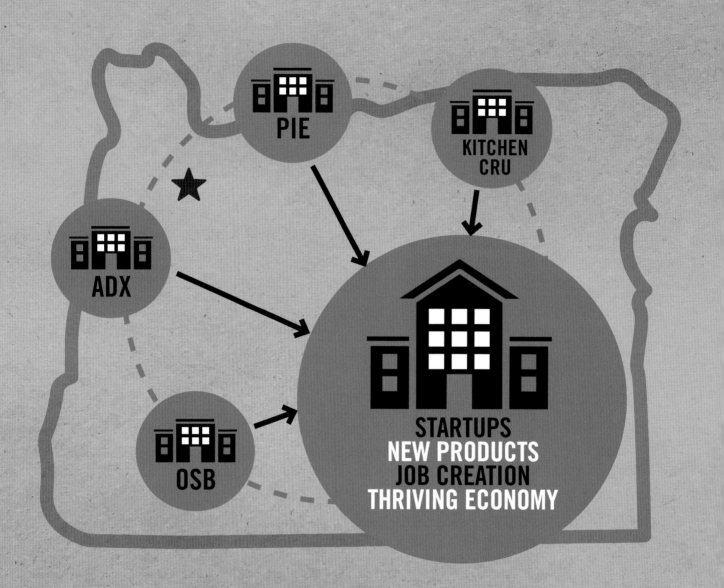

PIE

KITCHEN
CRU

ADX

OSB

STARTUPS
NEW PRODUCTS
JOB CREATION
THRIVING ECONOMY

INCUBATORS UNITE

ADX / adxportland.com OSB / oregonstoryboard.org
KITCHEN CRU / kitchencru.biz PIE / piepdx.com

INCUBATORS UNITE!

One of the many aspects of the makerspace model is its role as an incubator of new businesses. There are many incubator spaces in Portland that collectively serve a variety of industry sectors. Many of these spaces, like ADX, emerged during the recession of 2008 when many people were struggling to find work, and the trend continues as this book is being written.

Incubator spaces help accelerate ideas and bring products to market in a way that supports sustainable business growth. Like ADX, many of these spaces provide business consulting, access to capital, shared tools and equipment, and many other support systems that start-ups need to get off the ground.

Although the fast-growing tech start-up scene differs from the maker movement in many ways—the former driven more often by the bottom line than by artistic passion and connection to local culture—it is worth taking a closer look at some of the more innovative sharing-based models to see what's working.

At the center of the technology movement is the Portland Incubator Experiment (PIE). The tech equivalent of a makerspace, PIE is an imaginatively forward-thinking business incubator program that provides essential opportunities to small start-up tech companies. In 2009, Rick Turoczy was in the midst of planning a tech cooperative workspace in Portland and was experimenting with the idea of peer mentorship to help start-ups get their feet on the ground. He also interviewed a lot of start-ups for his blog, Silicon Florist. What he discovered was that "starting up was harder than it should have been." Nearly every new company was facing the same challenges, learning similar hard lessons on their own.

He decided it was time to give these businesses some help. A conversation with mega ad agency Wieden + Kennedy unearthed a shared interest: Wieden + Kennedy were interested in giving back to their community, but they didn't want to "just cut a check," explained Turoczy.

And so, PIE was born.

Their acceleration program runs only one series of classes per year, and start-ups have to apply and present their pitch to be accepted. The assistance they receive comes in several forms: a space to work, in the company of other emerging small businesses, for three months, which fosters peer-to-peer learning and creative brainstorming; access to experienced business and design mentors from Wieden + Kennedy; access to mentors who are past "graduates" of the PIE program; and $20,000 seed money to help the start-ups launch their businesses.

The approach of learning from each other's mistakes is a cornerstone of PIE's program. The weekly facilitated peer-mentorship meetings have only one instruction: participants have to talk about the things that haven't worked. Because chances are good that someone else in the group has had a similar experience and can share what they've tried and how they solved the problem. In short, mistakes are expected.

Here's another example of a successful local incubator. After twenty-six years working in the tech world, Michael Madigan decided to make a change and combine his love of food and wine with his skills in helping start-up businesses get on their feet. This was in 2008, when food carts were popping up all over Portland.

Madigan found that many start-ups "needed to learn to monetize" their business, he says. This wasn't exclusive to the food industry, but Madigan discovered there wasn't any specialized place for food-cart owners, caterers, and makers of specialty products

to get the mentorship they needed for their specific business challenges. In addition, there was a lack of available commercial kitchen space, which was a huge stumbling block for many food-related start-ups.

After talking to farmers and local food product producers at farmers' markets and food festivals, he had a better understanding of the challenges they faced. The challenge was that there was no existing model for business systems specific to food industry start-ups. And though there was a lot of overlap, there were also crucial differences between caterers, bakers, and makers of specialty products to take into consideration. So he built it slowly and relied on a lot of networking and collaborating. "Portland is unique, in that people are cooperative in everything." So he was able to establish a lot of helpful relationships with retail markets, designers, and marketing and accounting mentors to serve his program.

Madigan launched KitchenCru in 2008, and by now its reputation for incubating high-quality products is well established. When stores and markets learn that someone interested in being a vendor has gone through the KitchenCru program, there is an immediate "open door," says Madigan. The individual chef or producer still has to be accepted on his or her own merit, but the KitchenCru experience has proved to be a valuable and positive introduction.

Oregon Story Board is another well-known local success story. Their number one goal is to develop a cohesive mentorship and accelerated learning program for early-stage companies working in what program manager Krystal South calls "the other side of service"—those who are innovating digital storytelling products, strategies and services for entertainment and business purposes.

Digital storytelling encompasses film, video, animation, gaming, and other digital media. Oregon Story Board saw an opportunity to generate more jobs and economic impact through convergence and collaboration among these disciplines. There was a lack of mentorship programs that would teach small companies the business skills that would enable them to be more successful.

When Oregon Story Board's four-month accelerator program was conceived in 2013, the organization received funding from the state of Oregon for its potential to create new jobs in an evolving industry. When the first class received sixty-four applications—by word of mouth alone—Krystal South and executive director Jenny Moede knew they had tapped into something for which there was considerable interest and need.

The first three months of the program are devoted to developing good business skills. South says the best part has been the collaborations between participants from different business and nonprofit sectors. "It has proved our original question, of whether we could create a community network in a more meaningful way," to everyone's benefit.

The fourth month of the program is spent working on each company's presentation for Demo Day, where the founders share their stories, what they have learned and their accelerator milestones in front of interested members of the public and invited business representatives.

Demo Day turned out to be a huge success. "People were expecting prescriptive pitches but instead heard people's stories." They found these stories far more engaging and interesting than the more traditional business pitches they were used to seeing.

Because their business needs are as varied as the industries being served, Moede and South are hoping to be able to offer shorter courses for specific short-term questions and hurdles, maybe geared more to specific industries, with a focus on helping specific underrepresented groups, such as women and minorities.

Ultimately, they hope that Oregon Story Board will be able to act as a "hub for an entire web of digital storytelling industries."

EDUCATION

JOIN THE MOVEMENT!

One of the most exciting aspects of the maker movement is the nurturing of the next generation through a variety of nontraditional educational programs. As more and more young people move away from the antiquated educational institutions that focus primarily on college preparation (and that leave a large majority of kids unprepared for the modern workforce and riddled with debt) the maker movement—and more important, makerspaces—are stepping in to fill the gaps by helping young people develop skill sets that will enable them to make a living.

For the younger generation, the maker movement is about exploration and discovery—about messing around with parts and bits of things to understand in a hands-on way how something works. It has been proven through many scientific studies that allowing young people to work with their hands and figure things out on their own is critical to brain development. There is now a rallying cry to bring this type of learning back into K–12 education, and the maker movement is stepping up to provide the younger generation with more experiential of learning. At its core, the maker movement is all about lifelong learning. And makerspaces have evolved to meet people wherever they are in their process.

Exposing kids of all ages to the spirit of exploration and discovery that takes place at makerspaces is critical to young people's future success. Since the disappearance of shop class and the arts, students are very rarely given opportunities to work with their hands. And most students are never exposed to the idea that they could start their own company, design and develop their own product line, or make a good living in the manufacturing sector. In fact, manufacturing is still a dirty word to most people. But manufacturing has changed and it's not all about smokestacks and black lung. And young people need to learn that there are companies out there that are making

high-quality goods in safe work environments that value people and planet above profit. These companies represent the values of the younger generation and are in desperate need of a skilled and consistent workforce. In the words of one of the student groups that has visited ADX, "All everyone can talk about is college. It is nice to see what other options are out there. I love the idea of working with my hands and designing my own company."

In Portland, every public school is talking about wanting to integrate a makerspace into their campuses. Unfortunately, most of them have a limited understanding about what makes a makerspace and how to build community and develop curriculum that is relevant to twenty-first-century skills. Makerspaces take an incredible amount of time; they involve great risk and a considerable capital investment. They also cannot be bound by bureaucracy or institutional mediocrity. These barriers are fairly ominous for a large bureaucracy like a public school system to overcome, but

what's encouraging is that the administrators understand what an important resource a maker-space would be to their student body.

Portland Community College has been working hard to overcome some of these institutional barriers through the development of a fully equipped, full-spectrum education and training facility called the MakerSpace on their Sylvania campus. Students receive college credit, experience, and skills that qualify them to enter the world of manufacturing at all levels. In addition to completing coursework there, they can work on their own designs. This ability to experiment on small projects and to prototype ideas freely enables students to "fail forward versus fail backward," says instructor Gregg Meyer. In addition, because MakerSpace is an open drop-in lab, there is plenty of opportunity for brainstorming and peer mentoring. The tagline for MakerSpace is "Design. Make. Play." Having fun as a motivator, rather than a test, makes for a fast learning curve. "We're in the business of making dreams real," says Meyer.

Patrick Kraft and Gary Meyer have enthusiastic plans for the future, for extending the reach of programs like MakerSpace. They are working to expand their programs into high schools, including a teacher training and certification program. The teachers would then get a "maker cart" of supplies that enable real-life, hands-on learning for high school students.

"But why stop with high school?" Kraft and Meyer ask. "How do you get this down to the first, second, or third grade?"

Enter the Oregon Museum of Science and Industry (OMSI), whose mission is to "inspire curiosity through engaging science learning experiences, foster experimentation and the exchange of ideas, and stimulate informed action." **omsi.org**

When you enter the design lab at OMSI, you are likely to come upon a bustling scene. Kids may be making a stop-motion animation, exploring the physics of dominoes, or discovering the magic of a 3-D printer. Designed to engage people of all ages, the activities in the design lab are all about encouraging spatial thinking.

As kids experiment with different designs, "failure" is an important learning tool. The goal is to provide the tools, open-ended questions, and opportunity for collaborative learning so that the individual can eventually go farther than they thought they could. The key skills to creative discovery, as OMSI sees them, are "collaboration, communication and resilience."

The great thing is that it doesn't always have to be elaborate: one interactive exhibit (perhaps the favorite of museum visitors) is a box that shoots an upward blast of air; nearby is a supply of small cone-shaped paper cups and an abundance of scissors that can be used to create a paper cone that flies highest, farthest, and toward a specific target. Andrew Haight says this exhibit attracts people of all ages, but what is especially poignant and gratifying is that it doesn't rely on any common language to be a collaborative learning experience. With these simple tools and supplies, people are "making" and problem solving in a way that is simultaneously empowering and fun.

OMSI is midway through a multiyear grant from the National Science Foundation for an interactive exhibit titled Designing Our World. The question: How to encourage young women (preteen and teenage) in the sciences, including the field of engineering? What they've discovered is that girls respond better to an altruistic challenge rather than the more straightforward "making things"

The key skills to creative discovery, as OMSI sees them, are "collaboration, communication and resilience."

challenge that activate boys' interest. Although their motivation may be different, both will readily embrace the same tools and skills to reach the desired end. In a scenario where fresh water needs to be transported from one village to another across a river that has no bridge, young women suddenly become bridge builders!

OMSI also hosts the annual Mini Maker Faire, which encourages kids of all ages to explore, tinker, and invent. Maker Faires and Mini Maker Faires happen all over the country. and were the brainchild of Dale Dougherty. He and his team also launched MAKE magazine in 2005, which provides a catalyst for a tech-influenced DIY community that has come to be associated with the maker movement.

The movement is also engaging people in lifelong learning and showing the younger generation an alternative to our current education system. Makerspaces make learning engaging, interactive, hands on, and relevant. Working alongside people of all age groups and backgrounds teaches teamwork, active listening, and creative problem solving. Hand a kid a tape measure and she instantly understands why knowing how to add and subtract fractions is important. Introduce a young maker to a seasoned entrepreneur and watch her eyes light up as she starts to imagine herself starting her own business or making her own product line. Makerspaces teach people of all ages not only the skills of making but also life skills. In short, makerspaces are giving us the tools that we need to survive in a quickly changing world, helping us make more informed choices, teaching us another way of thinking about our consumption, and shaping the next generation's understanding and appreciation of manufactured goods.

We may not be there yet, but it's my greatest hope that a thriving makerspace is at the heart of every community around the world.

TRADE SCHOOLS
UNITED BICYCLE INSTITUTE

If you want to learn bikes, go to Portland.

United Bicycle Institute (UBI) attracts students from all over the world. "It is a very unique business," says Stephen Glass, manager of the Portland campus, since it's one of a few North American schools that offers coursework and certification in Bicycle Mechanics and Bicycle Frame Building. Veterans can use the Post-9/11 GI Bill to attend; the school also accepts students through vocational rehabilitation programs. UBI is a licensed private career school through Oregon State University, and as such it adheres to the same standards as other state schools, ensuring a truly professional education.

The original school, founded in 1981, is located in Ashland, Oregon. Due to increased demand, in 2009 a second school opened in Portland, enrolling four to five hundred students annually. Classes in Bicycle Mechanics are geared (no pun intended) to novice bike enthusiasts and professional mechanics alike, from those who simply want to learn about personal bike maintenance to those looking for more technical courses and vocational training. In the two-week courses on frame building, the students leave with their own custom-built frame and a new set of skills.

With such a diversity of students in attendance, the school has a challenge in terms of giving each individual what she or he needs. Glass credits UBI's success with its teachers, who have a combined two hundred years' experience. It's this depth and breadth of knowledge that enables such a wide range of students' needs to be met.

Many alternative educational programs are also feeding these maker collectives and the associated workforce that these growing companies are hiring. The United Bicycle Institute is training future bike builders, the American Barista & Coffee School is training future baristas and coffeepreneurs, the American Jewelers Institute is growing the next generation of jewelry designers, and the Portland Sewing school is training the future seamsters. These institutions are building a skilled workforce and creating future entrepreneurs in the creative industries.

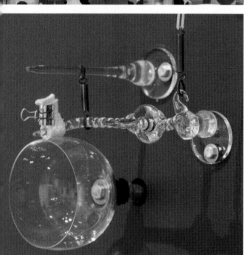

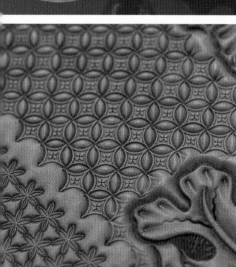

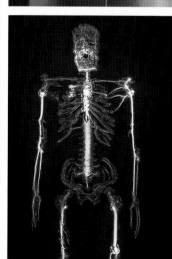

MUSEUMS
MUSEUM OF CONTEMPORARY CRAFT

Portland's Museum of Contemporary Craft has been at the forefront in its support of makers since its inception in 1937. Over the years it has changed its name, location, and programming, adapting to changes in the economy and interests of the public, but it has managed to retain its mission of craft at its core.

When it began as the Oregon Ceramic Studio (OCS), it was one of the few places on the West Coast where potters could purchase supplies and have access to a kiln. Grants from the Works Progress Administration provided funds to support the labor and materials needed to construct the original studio. During this time, OCS established the foundation of the studio movement in the Pacific Northwest and helped give an important start to many makers. Over the years, OCS expanded to include other kinds of craft, changed names a couple of times, and expanded its offerings to meet the demands of the city's deeply loyal community of makers. In 2007, it moved to its current Pearl District location and reopened as the Museum of Contemporary Craft. Since 2009, the museum has operated in partnership with the Pacific Northwest College of Art, providing unique and important opportunities for the next generation of makers.

Over the years the distinctions between "art" and "craft" have blurred and merged. Nicole Nathan says that the best explanation of the common ground of art, craft, and design comes from Karl Burkheimer, who is a member of the woodworking faculty at the Oregon College of Art and Craft. He explains that every maker is, at any given time, in the making process, whether that person is an artist, craftsperson, or designer. It requires the skills of all three to achieve excellence in making. Nathan sees that as one of the museum's roles: to recognize and champion the maker community and the "rigorous approach" and skill sets that lead to excellence.

Another key role for museums is to act as an interface between the makers and the community. Exhibits become places where historical pieces from the collection and modern ones are juxtaposed to tell the narrative of an object. For example, in the 2013 exhibit Object Focus: The Bowl, visitors were invited to look at common objects in different contexts, to engage and reflect in an atmosphere of exploration, where there is no single right answer. Going forward, says Nathan, the museum will continue to ask, "How can we discuss and pose questions about art, craft, and design in an open-ended and exploratory way?"

Rulers
Measur
Needles
Pins + C
Bobbins
Cutter +
Pattern
Thread

ADX CLASS
CUB

SUPPORT SERVICES

In addition to their need for visibility, marketing assistance, education, and community, makers sometimes need funds to get their project launched. Several organizations offer makers professional assistance and access to capital during their initial phase of growth. Many of our new local manufacturers have worked with the Oregon Manufacturing Extension Partnership to expand and streamline their operations. Plywerk and Spooltown have gone through Portland Community College's Small Business Management program to gain better insight into growing their profits and controlling their expenses. Mercy Corps Northwest and Albina Opportunities Corporation provided ADX with a start-up loan that would have been nearly impossible to get from a traditional bank. Black Star Bags and Hot Winter Hot Sauce have used Community Sourced Capital to raise zero-interest community loans for expanding their product lines, and Craft3, a community-development financial institution, has provided loans for many local start-ups throughout the Pacific Northwest since 1994.

MERCY CORPS NORTHWEST /
mercycorpsnw.org

OREGON MANUFACTURING EXTENSION PROGRAM /
omep.org

PORTLAND COMMUNITY COLLEGE /
pcc.edu/climb/small-business/growing

ALBINA OPPORTUNITIES CORPS /
albinaopportunities.org

COMMUNITY SOURCED CAPITAL /
communitysourcedcapital.com

CONSUMERS AS INVESTORS
BUY LOCAL

Consumers are the maker movement's biggest investor and the best way to engage and educate the community about the maker movement is at the point of purchase. Many makers sell their products themselves rather than selling wholesale to a retailer. Oftentimes, direct sales to consumers are a result of necessity because the margins are too tight to wholesale their products. Selling online is a logical option, but makers don't always have the business savvy or resources to create a consumer website. Online collectives like Portland Made and retailers like MadeHere PDX have stepped in to help.

Modern consumers are not only interested in the product; they are also interested in the story behind the product—and, more specifically, the story of the person whose hands made the product. By promoting locally produced products, Portland Made and MadeHere PDX help makers reach wider audiences and also enable them to tell their stories and establish an emotional connection to consumers.

A great tool for testing new products before taking them to market is crowdfunding platforms. My favorite among the many options out there now is Crowd Supply. Recent successes include the projects USB Armory: Open Source USB Stick Computer; *A Weather Walked In* photography book; and the Portland Press, a French press that fits a mason jar. According to Crowd Supply founder and CEO Joshua Lifton, "As engineers and designers, we know the challenges of going from idea to reality, and all the important details in between. We built Crowd Supply from the ground up to handle as many of those details as possible so you can focus on your vision." A product designer makes one product, puts it on a crowdfunding site like Crowd Supply, and quickly and affordably determines the demand for the product. If the product is a success, then the designer can go into production, producing only what has been ordered. If it is not a success, then the designer has saved a lot of time and money, as well as precious natural resources. Unlike Kickstarter and other crowdfunding sites, Crowd Supply is deeply invested in the long-term success of the products and companies it supports. From up-front marketing and videography to long-term sales and distribution through their online storefront, Crowd Supply assists

BY PROMOTING LOCALLY PRODUCED PRODUCTS, PORTLAND MADE AND MADEHERE PDX HELP MAKERS REACH WIDER AUDIENCES AND ALSO ENABLE THEM TO TELL THEIR STORIES AND ESTABLISH AN EMOTIONAL CONNECTION TO CONSUMERS.

its clients through the entire process of taking a new product to market.

For makers who want to pursue the more traditional route of selling their goods through retailers in a brick-and-mortar space, there is no better place than the MadeHere PDX store in downtown Portland. With extensive experience curating the modern retail environment, MadeHere takes the pressure off makers by selling their wares for them.

A true celebration of Portland's maker scene, MadeHere PDX is dedicated to showcasing excellent craftsmanship and a commitment to quality. Interestingly, sales are about split between locals and out-of-town visitors looking to take a piece of Portland back to their communities.

The vendors MadeHere chooses feature items that are "more than the sum of their parts," says co-owner John Connor. The vendors are generally not in the early stages of their business but are instead producing in a volume that can consistently supply a consignment retail space. When MadeHere

PDX first opened, it had approximately forty vendors. By spring of 2015 that number had doubled, and it doesn't show signs of stopping anytime soon. Connor stresses that MadeHere PDX "wants to be a retail partner" with their makers to help them succeed. For some makers, this is their first foray into being in a retail location; Connor sees this as akin to a beta-testing experience—MadeHere is able to give makers specific feedback on their products based on what they hear directly and indirectly from customers. This can be extremely valuable to makers who have not had access to this kind of marketing and sales feedback before.

MadeHere PDX also operates an online shop, which has proven to be a successful pairing, especially for follow-up purchases for travelers who can't easily return to the shop.

CROWD SUPPLY / crowdsupply.com
MADEHERE PDX / madeherepdx.com

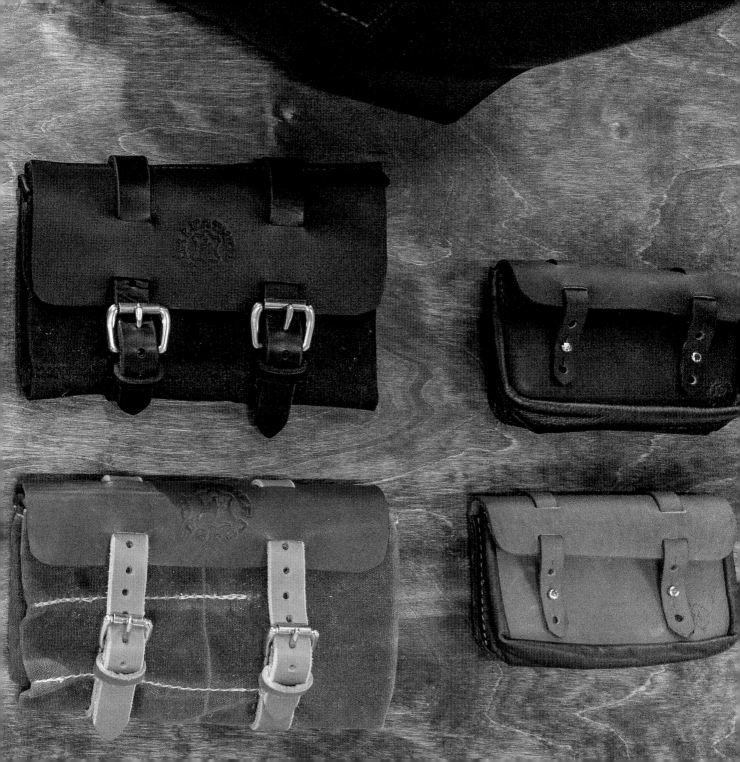

THE FUTURE
OF THE
MAKER MOVEMENT

BUILDING A GLOBAL NETWORK

The maker movement is growing rapidly around the world. ADX gets at least five calls a week from people who want to know how to start a makerspace. Inquiries come from Japan, South Africa, Europe, and Australia, as well as from cities across North and South America. ADX is helping communities with local culture building, place making, and economic-development strategies by working with them to identify and tie the pieces of their local maker movement together. This includes helping them start makerspaces and maker collectives that encourage the sharing of space, knowledge, and tools, while helping build resiliency into their community economic-development strategy.

In Portland, there is huge potential for ADX-like incubator spaces for each Portland Made Collective industry sector. We would love to be part of starting an ADX specific to the fashion industry, the bike industry, and the craft-brewing industry. By combining forces with other successful incubator spaces, we could create an even stronger economic-development strategy, one that not only fosters new businesses but also trains up the workforce needed to support the rapid growth of these industry sectors. Maker collectives continue to pop up all the time. As of the writing of this book, Portland Made is working on a real estate concept called "the Industrial Grange" that will work with existing maker collectives and create new ones that are all tied together under one brand: Portland Made. Warehouses will be labeled with the Portland Made Collective (PMC) brand, bringing more visibility to the movement.

City economic-development leaders should pay attention to this trend and find ways to support these types of spaces by providing free or discounted rent on a variety of manufacturing space, funding for instructors and mentors on both the making and business side, and funding for capital improvements, especially equipment and tooling. Even small infusions of money can make a big difference to the artisanal manufacturing economy in Portland. And these small investments in shared incubator spaces across many of Portland's creative industry sectors will lead to the acceleration of new local products going to market.

There is also a need for a certification system for sustainably manufactured goods, something like the green building industry's LEED (Leadership in Energy and Environmental Design) certification or the agriculture industry's organic certification. This certification would need to be handled with care, as infrastructure and associated costs of certification could create unnecessary barriers to entry, but it is a topic that merits further research and discussion. Brooklyn Made has an interesting certification system that could easily be applied to other cities around the country.

The lessons we have learned since 2010 are worth reflecting on collectively as we look to help other cities support and grow their own maker movement. Affordability is the primary concern. As real estate prices continue to rise, we are in serious danger of gentrifying our culture builders right out of the city. We saw this happen in Portland's NW warehouse district, which was rebranded as the Pearl District during the gentrification process. Back in the early 2000s, the old warehouse buildings were occupied by artists, but as soon as the streetcar and accompanying real estate developers moved in, the warehouses were torn down and the creatives had to move out. Many of them moved to affordable eastside neighborhoods and started unintentionally gentrifying those. There is a long-standing trend of artists and other culture makers occupying lower-rent neighborhoods, and then the more mainstream culture follows close behind, raising property values and pushing the artists out to new places and starting the whole process over again. Only local government policies can stop this from happening, and there are some great examples from cities across the country.

As the maker movement in Portland continues to grow and gain attention, real estate developers are getting in on the action. This is not always a good thing, as property owners often demand higher rents and sales prices for marginal real estate. This type of speculation is currently an issue in Portland's Central Eastside Industrial District (CEID). With a long history of manufacturing, the CEID has been experiencing rapid growth over the past seven to ten years as warehouses are being converted to creative office space. Valuable manufacturing infrastructure is being lost in the process. Although the city understands the importance of the maker movement—not only for job creation but also for culture building—its administrators have not been able to contain the problem. They see the brewers, the bike manufacturers, the fashion designers, and the wide variety of craftsmen and women who add dimension, beauty, and vitality to our city, and they know that Portland makers are drawing tourists from around the world, but their hands are tied. There is currently no mechanism in Portland for the city to prevent real estate prices from pushing manufacturing out.

This is a huge problem, because creatives are the catalysts for cities of the future. They nurture culture and ensure that cities are not just bastions of homogenous consumers. There is much to be learned from the conservation movement, which has found ways to protect land from speculation. Farm trusts and land trusts are used as mechanisms to conserve and protect land for food production, wetland conservation, and other wildland protection purposes. In urban areas, an industrial land trust could be created to protect urban land for certain uses that keep the rents affordable for culture makers. A Portland industrial trust is badly needed if we are going to protect the things we value. If we're not careful, intentional, and forward-thinking about our preserving this movement, there will be nothing to distinguish Portland from any other city in the country.

The Portland Maker Movement model could be applied to other cities around the country depending on the various cultural, educational, and economic-development activities they want to support. ADX has begun to organize training summits to help leaders from communities around the globe understand how makerspaces and maker collectives work. Starting a makerspace and sparking a maker movement are not easy—they require an incredible amount of time, commitment, financial resources, and a tolerance for risk. Both actions require people with a commitment to local culture and values and a strong desire to preserve and protect what makes your city great.

Makerspaces will be different in each city, and depending on the players involved, the model

will be different in each place. They are culture-based businesses that are informed by local economic needs, history, natural surroundings, arts and culture, environmental awareness, community activism, and more. The business model could be private, nonprofit, governmental, or some creative combination of all three. But regardless of the form, every city around the world should have a makerspace.

The point is: Makerspaces are vital—to our communities and to our planet. They inspire creativity; supply people with the tools and skills and motivation to pursue their dreams; contribute to urban culture; promote ethical buying; and are just fun, dynamic places to boot. But if we want them, we're going to have to get serious—and creative—about supporting them. The good news is that we can all make a difference by spending our dollars wisely. That momentum will hopefully encourage local governments to take notice and throw their support behind preserving and further growing a movement that will truly change the world.

AFTERWORD

GET INVOLVED. JOIN THE MOVEMENT!

The maker movement is changing the way we learn and reminding people about the power of working in community. Technology, despite its incredible power to connect people instantly all over the world, often leaves us feeling disconnected and alone.

There's something deeply satisfying about working with our hands, reconnecting with the process, and building a strong community and spirit of collaboration.

Makerspaces are alive with sounds and smells and visual stimulation. The most common thing people tell me is how ADX makes them feel. They may have looked at our website a thousand times, but walking through the front door and having all of their senses activated simultaneously in such a dynamic environment thrills people. As they tour the space, people are awed by the variety of projects in progress: wooden spheres, boats of all shapes and sizes, snowboards and surfboards, arduino-activated installations, food trucks, furniture, straight razors, lighting, and more. It inevitably makes them want to get started making something. And this is the magic of the maker movement. Anyone and everyone can be involved.

Many people would like to make things but have no idea how to get started. Makerspaces can help those people turn their dreams into a reality. All they have to do is show up. People can hang out and talk to each other and show each other different ways of looking at a project. Seeing the world through the eyes of others is important to the creative process. It is a magical thing to witness the moment when people let go of their insecurities and just give themselves over to the creative process.

Even people who do not want to make things find ADX exciting because it is so full of ideas and experimentation. All of us, whether we are artists or not, love getting an inside look at the artistic process. Makerspaces give everyone access to that mysterious creative exploration. Seeing how things are made gives us a deeper appreciation for the process—for the people behind the process; for the materials involved; and for the sounds, the feel, and the touch of how things are made. In short, it gives objects meaning.

If the public visited the nation's industrial farms and slaughterhouses to see how animals are raised and killed, many of us would ask more questions and demand better conditions. Many more of us would likely never eat meat again. It's no different when it comes to the factories in China. You only have to watch the documentary film Manufactured Landscapes once to start questioning your consumer habits. By exposing the process of how things are made, we can start to change our habits. All of the little choices we make about how we spend our money add up. As consumers, we have the greatest power to shape and grow the maker movement. As the saying goes, knowledge is power.

Inform yourselves. Get involved. Join the movement!

STOP TALKING

START
MAKING

OPEN HABIT

OPEN HABIT

ALL DAY, EVERYDAY

CONTRIBUTING WRITERS

Peggy Acott is a fifth-generation Oregonian and has been writing for what seems like her entire life. Before she could write, she would dictate stories to a willing parent, adding illustrations and stapling them together in an early effort at self-publishing. Her work has appeared in *Portland Outsider*, *Edible Portland*, *Alltopia*, and *Savor: An Anthology*; online at Cooking Up a Story, Cactus Heart Press, Communal Table, and the Portland Made website. Please visit her online at **peggyacott. wordpress.com** and **storytoceremony.wordpress.com**

ADX communications director **Matt Preston** was born in a small country town in Florida. Constantly on the search for new adventure, good music, and amazing people, Matt has found his way into the sawdust-covered arms of ADX. He believes in a style of marketing and sales that focuses on smiling, laughing, and being honest. Work aside, he enjoys playing his guitar to an audience (the walls of his room), telling stories to those who will listen, and learning to turn wood in the shop.

EDITOR

Christina Henry de Tessan has worked in publishing for nearly two decades, toiling away as both an in-house editor (Chronicle Books, Seal Press) and a freelance writer before joining Girl Friday Productions, an editorial, writing, and design firm. She loves all aspects of the book business— writing, editing, research, reading, and, of course, other people who share her passion for words. Originally from San Francisco, she enjoyed stints in Seattle and Paris before finally landing in the foodie-hipster mecca of Portland, Oregon. She loves indulging in dim sum in San Francisco, dress shopping in Brooklyn, late-night book browsing at Powell's in Portland, and doing just about anything in Paris.

BOOK DESIGN & ILLUSTRATION

Jen Cogliantry is a New York–based art director and graphic designer. After graduating from Brighton Polytechnic in the south of England and a five-year stint with London-based publisher DBP, she relocated to New York City 1997 to set up 3+Co., a specialized design agency developing branding and packaging for companies that include the Nonesuch Records, HarperCollins

Publishers, Metropolitan Opera, and the Japanese Chamber of Commerce. In 2008, she packed her family into a 1958 vintage camper and drove west to Portland, where she honed her commercial and branding design skills. Now living in Brooklyn with husband, Michael Cogliantry, and daughter, Tanner, Jen freelances for clients such as Reebok, Sterling Publishing and Ecotrust. Her work can be seen via **jencogliantry.com**. Also a maker, she recently launched a line handcrafted accessories. Visit **jencogliantry-handmade.com**.

PHOTOGRAPHY

Aaron Lee is a Portland-based commercial photographer specializing in capturing moments, feelings, and emotions through the interplay of light and shadows. Aaron was born and raised in northeast Portland and has a deep affinity for helping the local business community. He left the high corporate ranks of advertising at Wieden + Kennedy, among others, to pursue his lifelong passion of photography and opened his studio in the Pearl District in 2012. His website is **aaronleephotography.com**.

Josh Doll is an LA native who has spent his twenties in the Pacific Northwest; his loyalties are to the West Coast. Having spent his youth as a freelance designer and illustrator for various punk record labels and small businesses, he came to ADX in late 2011 and started pushing a broom. Soon after, he co-founded Band (a creative studio he operates with his good pal Zach) within the shop. Still a punk at heart, Josh believes in the power of collaboration and community over that of competition and exclusivity.

REFERENCES

PG 14 /
Joe Cortright, *"Portland: Hardly 'A Retirement Community for the Young,'"* CityLab, September 17, 2014, citylab.com/housing/2014/09/portland-hardly-a-retirement-community-for-the-young/380381.

PG 30 /
Kim Gittleson, *"US Manufacturing: The Rise of the Niche Manufacturer,"* BBC Online, February 20, 2015, bbc.com/news/business-31527888.

PG 130 /
omsi.org/about

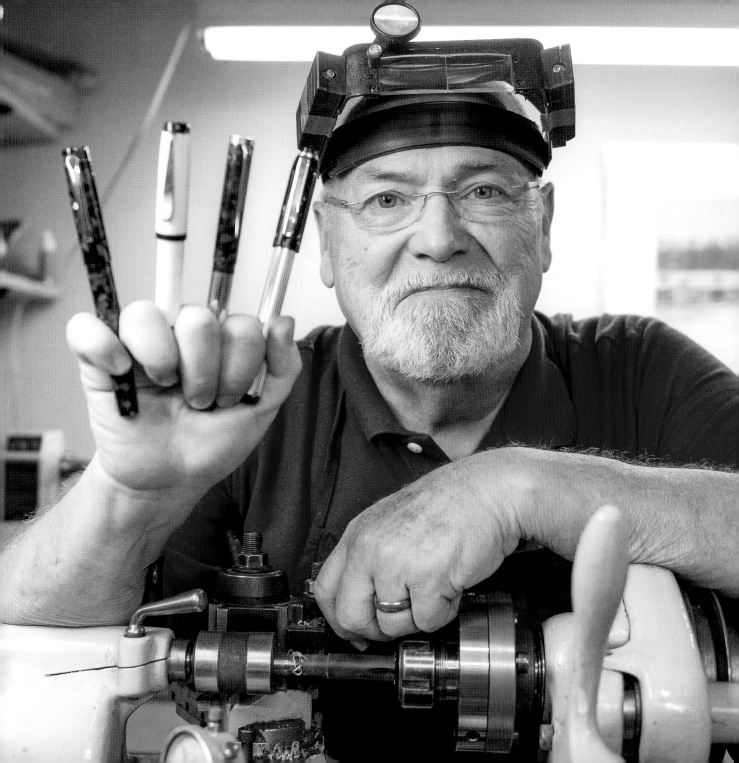

MAKERS GOTTA MAKE

As the founder and owner of ADX, I have had the good fortune to be at the helm of an extraordinary experiment in urban life. Portland is at the forefront of a New American Manufacturing Revolution, and ADX has been an important catalyst in shaping the handcrafted goods movement. I am constantly asked-by Portlanders, non-Portlanders, politicians, non-profits, and other creatives who want to start similar movements in their own cities—what this creative renaissance looks like. This book is the answer. —*Kelley Roy*, founder of ADX Portland

ISBN 978-0-692-46892-0

53500>

9 780692 468920